Reflections

Ancient Civilizations

Homework and Practice Book

Grade 6

Harcourt
SCHOOL PUBLISHERS

Orlando   Austin   New York   San Diego   Toronto   London

Visit *The Learning Site!*
www.harcourtschool.com

Printed in the United States of America

ISBN 978-0-15-341481-7

30   0928 17 16

4500602191

Reflections

The activities in this book reinforce social studies concepts and skills in Harcourt School Publishers' *Reflections: Ancient Civilizations*. There is one activity for each lesson and skill. In addition to activities, this book also contains reproductions of the graphic organizers that appear in the chapter reviews in the Student Edition. Study guides for student review are also provided. Reproductions of the activity pages appear with answers in the Teacher Edition.

Contents

·UNIT 1· EARLY HUMANKIND

·UNIT 2· MESOPOTAMIA, EGYPT, AND KUSH

·UNIT 3· THE ANCIENT HEBREWS

·UNIT 6· THE DEVELOPMENT OF ROME

The Distant Past

DIRECTIONS Read about each fossil or tool. Write the term from the box that identifies the type of hominid it most likely came from or was used by.

australopithecine	*Homo erectus*	*Homo habilis*

1 This arm bone comes from a female hominid in eastern Africa. It is believed that she lived about 3 million years ago.

The bone probably belonged to _____.

2 This leg bone comes from Asia. Archaeological theories about migration would indicate that this hominid's species

is _____.

3 This jawbone from Africa dates to the Paleolithic era. It is smaller than older ones from the region, so it probably

belonged to _____.

DIRECTIONS Complete each statement to tell about the study of early humans.

4 Artifacts such as tools and pottery help archaeologists learn about _____

_____

5 Archaeologists compare human bones and fossils from different time periods to

_____

6 Excavation sites are divided into grids because _____

_____

7 Scientists believe that *Homo erectus* began to migrate beyond Africa because

_____

8 The bones of *Homo habilis* were first discovered by _____

CALIFORNIA STANDARDS HSS 6.1, 6.1.1

Early Modern Humans

DIRECTIONS Answer the following questions to tell how *Homo sapiens* differed from other hominids.

What does *Homo sapiens* mean?

_____

What are three ways that *Homo sapiens's* greater intelligence helped this hominid?

_____

_____

_____

_____

_____

_____

In what kinds of dwellings did *Homo sapiens* live?

_____

What did male *Homo sapiens* do?

_____

What did female *Homo sapiens* do?

_____

Why did *Homo sapiens* live in groups?

_____

_____

_____

_____

_____

Why did *Homo sapiens* have to learn to adapt to the environment?

_____

How did *Homo sapiens* depend on animals?

_____

_____

CALIFORNIA STANDARDS HSS 6.1, 6.1.1; 6.1.2; CS 3   *(continued)*

Name _____ Date _____

DIRECTIONS Complete the web to show why early hunter-gatherer societies often moved instead of settling in one place.

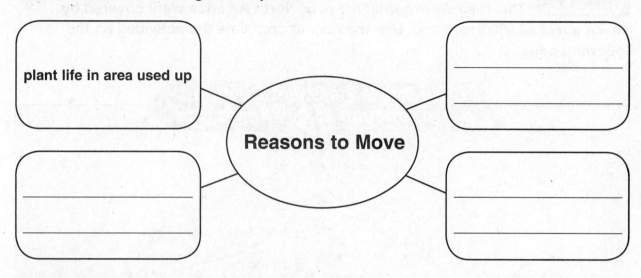

| plant life in area used up | | **Reasons to Move** | | |

DIRECTIONS On the map, locate and label the continents and other places in the box below to which early peoples migrated from Africa.

Australia	Alaska	North America	Asia
South America	Indonesia	Europe	

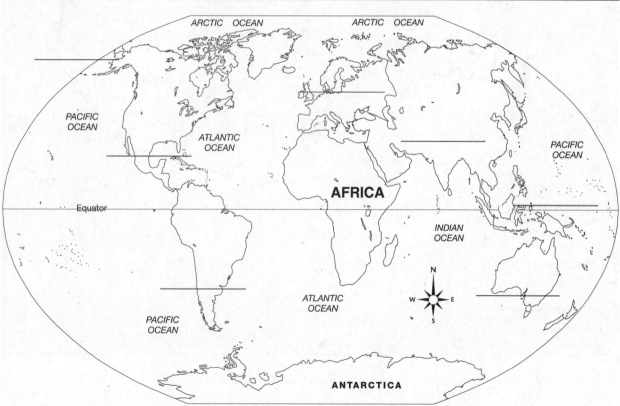

Skills: Use Latitude and Longitude

DIRECTIONS This map shows what areas of North America were covered by an ice sheet 15,000 years ago. Use the map to complete the activities on the following page.

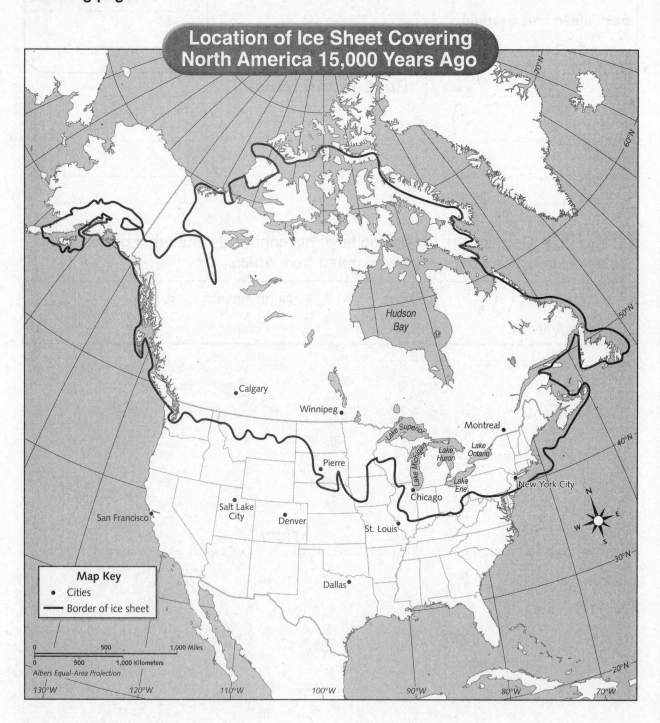

Location of Ice Sheet Covering North America 15,000 Years Ago

Map Key
- • Cities
- — Border of ice sheet

0 ___ 500 ___ 1,000 Miles
0 ___ 500 ___ 1,000 Kilometers
Albers Equal-Area Projection

CALIFORNIA STANDARDS HSS 6.1, 6.1.3; CS 3

(continued)

Name _____ Date _____

1 Which present-day city is located nearest to 40°N, 110°W?

_____

2 Was this region covered by ice 15,000 years ago? _____

3 Which present-day city is closest to 50°N, 100°W?

_____

4 Was this region covered by ice 15,000 years ago? _____

5 Which present-day body of water does 60°N cross?

_____

6 Was this region covered by ice 15,000 years ago? _____

7 Which present-day city is closest to 40°N, 90°W?

_____

8 Was this region covered by ice 15,000 years ago? _____

9 Choose another present-day city. Write its name and give its location, using

latitude and longitude. _____

_____

10 Was this region covered by ice 15,000 years ago? _____

Hunters and Gatherers of the World

DIRECTIONS Read each statement about an early hunter-gatherer society. From the box below, choose the name of the region in which the group lived, and write it in the space provided. If the statement can apply to more than one region, write *more than one*.

Africa	Europe	North America
Asia and the Pacific		South America

1 _____ Archaeological findings at the small river valley of Monte Verde show dwellings made from wood and animal skins and the use of fireplaces for cooking.

2 _____ Early fishing societies along the Baltic Sea created specialized tools such as harpoons, nets, and spears to adapt to their environment.

3 _____ The early hunters of Nelson's Bay Cave most likely used bows and arrows to kill antelope, pigs, and other wild animals.

4 _____ The rich diversity of plant and animal life here gave the early hunters and gatherers a varied and plentiful diet.

5 _____ The hunters and gatherers in this region created wood spears topped with Clovis points to hunt large Ice Age animals.

6 _____ As early hunters and gatherers traveled in this region, they found the terrain could change dramatically. This caused them to develop new ways of living.

7 _____ The use of clay pots for food and water storage is believed to have begun in this region.

8 _____ Archaeologists have found that some early societies that depended mostly on plants for food lived in caves in one of this region's rain forests.

9 _____ Because plants and wild animals were abundant along the Euphrates River, the population of Abu Hureyra grew to more than 300 people.

CALIFORNIA STANDARDS HSS 6.1, 6.1.1, 6.1.2; HI1 *(continued)*

Name _____ Date _____

Imagine that you are going to present a talk comparing two early hunter-gatherer societies. Choose two continental regions, and complete the organizer to show how they were alike and different.

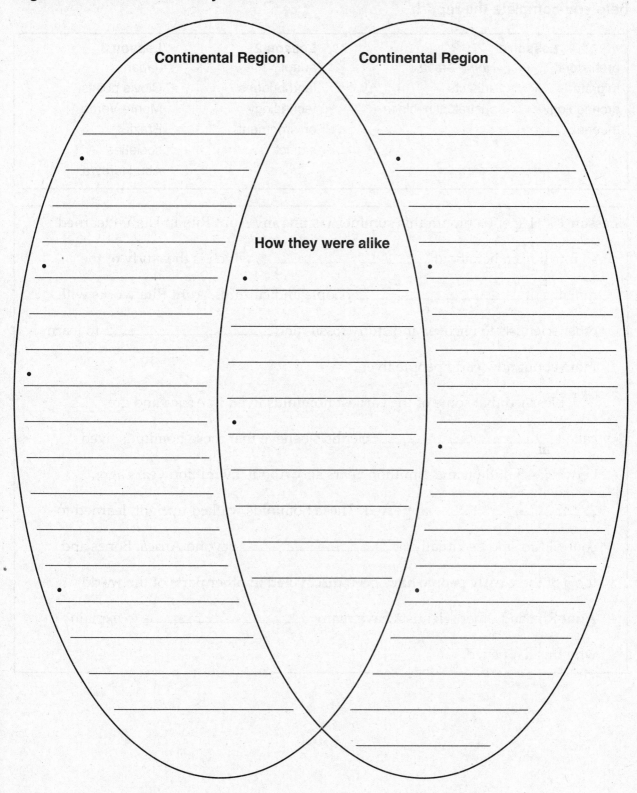

Continental Region

Continental Region

How they were alike

Chapter 1

Name _____   Date _____

Study Guide

DIRECTIONS Fill in the missing information in this report. Use the terms below to help you complete the report.

Lesson 1		Lesson 2	Lesson 3
prehistoric	*Homo erectus*	adapt	Japan
migrated	artifacts	land bridges	Clovis points
archaeology	australopithecines	technology	Monte Verde
theories		environment	Brazil
		extinct	societies
			Abu Hureyra

Lesson 1   I spent a month this summer visiting my Aunt Rita in Utah. I learned so much from her about _____, which is the study of the remains of _____ people and cultures. Aunt Rita works with other scientists to uncover and study fossils and _____ to learn more about how early people lived.

I learned that some of the earliest hominids lived in Africa and are called _____. Scientists believe that these hominids lived between 4.5 million and 1 million years ago. About 1.9 million years ago, _____ appeared. These hominids walked upright, learned to control fire, and eventually _____ beyond Africa. Bones and tools of these early people have been discovered in other parts of the world. Aunt Rita and other scientists have many _____ to explain why this happened.

CALIFORNIA STANDARDS HSS 6.1, 6.1.1, 6.1.2, 6.1.3   *(continued)*

8 ▪ Homework and Practice Book   Use after reading Chapter 1, pages 14–37.

Name _____ Date _____

Lesson 2   Aunt Rita says that scientists believe that early humans continued

to develop and that by 200,000 years ago, *Homo sapiens* appeared. *Homo*

sapiens's greater intelligence helped them to create _____ such

as special tools and weapons.

   Homo sapiens lived in small groups of family members, who worked

together to _____ to their surroundings. They gathered and

ate the useful plants in their _____ and then moved on to

new areas. Aunt Rita says that many of the animals they depended on, such as

mastodons and giant sloths, are now _____.

   I learned that changes in Earth's climate helped *Homo sapiens* move all over

the world. In some areas, _____ were uncovered that allowed

Homo sapiens to migrate to other continents.

Lesson 3   Aunt Rita told me about how scientists have found remains of early

hunter-gatherer _____ around the world. One large settle-

ment, _____, was located near the Euphrates River. In

the United States, tips of spears, called _____, have been

found all over. The earliest clay pots are believed to have been made in

_____.

   Aunt Rita has really opened up a new world of thinking for me. Some day,

I would like to visit some of the many South American prehistoric sites that

have been found in Peru and _____. In one site in southern

Chile, called _____, scientists have found that early people

there had houses with fireplaces.

READING SOCIAL STUDIES:
MAIN IDEA AND DETAILS

(Focus Skill) **The World's Early People**

DIRECTIONS Complete this graphic organizer to show that you can identify the main idea and supporting details of how early people adapted to their environments.

Main Idea and Details

Main Idea

Early humans adapted to a variety of environments.

Details

Early humans built temporary shelters out of dried mud and tree branches.		

CALIFORNIA STANDARDS HSS 6.1, 6.1.1, 6.1.2, 6.1.3

10 ▪ Homework and Practice Book   Use after reading Chapter 1, pages 14–37.

Producing Food

DIRECTIONS Number the sentences below in the order in which the events occurred.

_____ The end of the Ice Age brought warmer temperatures to many parts of the world.

_____ Permanent settlements and communities formed as people developed knowledge of farming.

_____ People in southwestern Asia began to domesticate plants and animals.

_____ Most people traveled from area to area, surviving as hunters and gatherers.

_____ People, plants, and animals spread farther north and south beyond the equator.

DIRECTIONS Describe the effect of farming on each topic listed on the right.

Livestock

_____

_____

Settlement

_____

_____

RESULTS OF FARMING

Land Ownership

_____

_____

Surplus

_____

_____

Rules

_____

_____

CALIFORNIA STANDARDS HSS 6.1, 6.1.3; CS 1, HI 2

Skills: Read Parallel Time Lines

DIRECTIONS Use the time line to complete the activities on the following page.

Discovery of Important Human Fossils

Africa
1850   1900   1950   2000

1921
Homo sapiens
found in Zambia
by Aleš Hrdlička

1936
Australopithecine
found in South
Africa by Robert
Broom

1959
Australopithecine found
in Tanzania by Mary
and Louis Leakey

1969
Australopithecine
found in Kenya
by Richard Leakey

1974
Australopithecine
found in Ethiopia
by Maurice Taleb
and Donald
Johanson

1924
Australopithecine
found in
South Africa by
Raymond Dart

1947
Australopithecine
found in
South Africa by
Raymond Dart

1967
Australopithecine
found in Ethiopia by
Camille Arambourg,
Yves Coppens, and
F. Clark Howell

1972
Homo habilis found
in Kenya by
Richard Leakey

1978
Australopithecine
found in Tanzania
by Mary Leakey

Asia
1850   1900   1950   2000

1891
Homo erectus
found in Indonesia
by Eugène Dubois

1927
Homo erectus
found in China by
Davidson Black

1931
Homo sapiens found in
Indonesia by C. ter Harr
and W. F. F. Oppenoorth

Europe
1850   1900   1950   2000

1856
Homo sapiens found
in Germany by
Johann Fuhlrott and
Herman Schaaffhausen

1868
Cro-Magnon
found in France
by Louis Lartet

1907
Homo erectus
found in
Germany by Otto
Schoetensack

1933
Homo sapiens found
in Germany by
Fritz Berckhemer

1935
Homo sapiens
found in England
by A. T. Marston

CALIFORNIA STANDARDS HSS 6.1, 6.1.2; CS 1, HI 2, 5 (*continued*)

Name _____ Date _____

1 The time line covers a period of how many years? _____

2 Describe where and when the earliest human fossil was found. _____

_____

3 According to the time line, on which continent were the most fossils of *Homo*

erectus found? _____

4 According to the time line, when and where was *Homo habilis* first found?

_____

5 The first discovery of *Homo sapiens* was in 1856, in Europe. Tell how many years
passed before the next important discovery of *Homo sapiens* and where the fossil

was found. _____

_____

6 Tell who first found the fossil of *Homo erectus* and when and where it was found.

_____

_____

7 According to the time line, on which continent were fossils of

australopithecines found? _____

8 Which type of fossil was found only in Europe? _____

9 Write a sentence that describes the time period during which the most fossil

discoveries were made. _____

_____

10 According to the time line, which species had the largest number of important

fossil discoveries? _____

Forming Complex Societies

DIRECTIONS Match each early culture or community with the clue that describes it. Write the name from the box in the space provided.

Bandkeramik	Çatal Hüyük	Yangshao
Mehrgarh	Abu Hureyra	

1 _____ In what is now Turkey, this ancient community developed trade around obsidian, which was used for making tools.

2 _____ These early people developed farming in northern China by creating terraces in the sides of hills and mountains.

3 _____ This farming culture's name comes from the type of pottery the people made.

4 _____ Cotton was grown and used for cloth in this ancient village, located in the Indus Valley.

5 _____ This successful early settlement in southwestern Asia grew into a faming village with permanent dwellings.

DIRECTIONS Complete the flowchart about how early farming societies progressed. Write a sentence to describe each step in the chart.

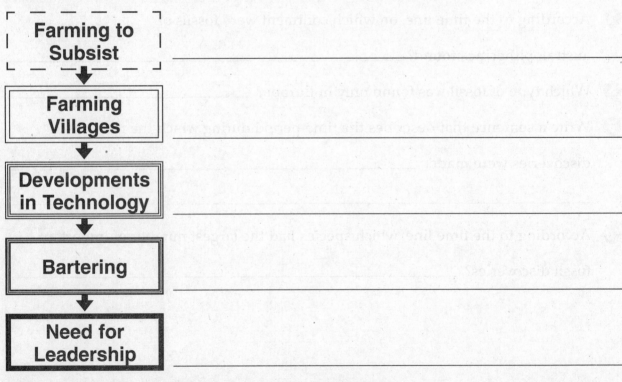

Farming to Subsist _____

↓

Farming Villages _____

↓

Developments in Technology _____

↓

Bartering _____

↓

Need for Leadership _____

 CALIFORNIA STANDARDS HSS 6.1, 6.1.2, 6.1.3, 6.2.2; HI 2

Skills: Use Relief and Elevation Maps

DIRECTIONS Use the maps of present-day Tanzania on the following page to complete the activities below.

1 Describe how the two maps of present-day Tanzania are alike and different.

_____

_____

_____

_____

2 List the mountains in Tanzania in order from highest to lowest elevation.

_____

_____

_____

3 If you traveled from Dodoma to Dar es Salaam, would you be at a higher, a lower, or the same elevation?

_____

_____

4 Locate the city of Mwanza. In what elevation range does it lie?

_____

5 How does the elevation of Tanzania's eastern border differ from the elevation of the country's western border?

_____

_____

_____

CALIFORNIA STANDARDS HSS 6.1; CS 3   *(continued)*

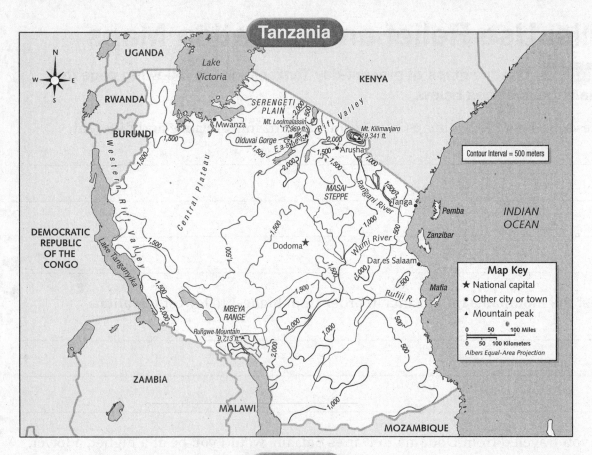

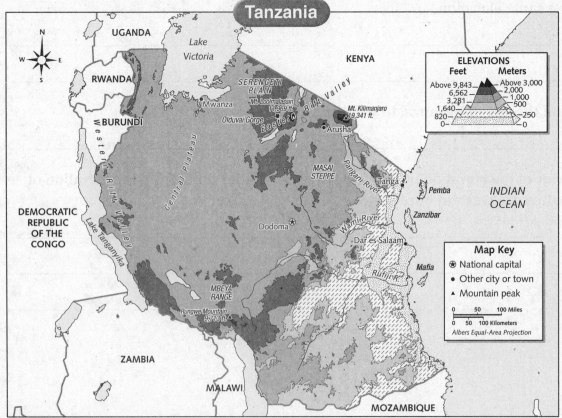

CALIFORNIA STANDARDS HSS 6.1, 6.1.2; CS 3

Use after reading Chapter 2, Skill Lesson, pages 62–63.

Building Communities

DIRECTIONS As early cities and civilizations developed, people formed ways of building and supporting communities. Write a description of each of the following developments in early cities.

1 Division of labor: _____

_____

2 Social classes: _____

_____

3 Taxation: _____

_____

DIRECTIONS Read the descriptions that follow. Use the terms in the box to identify what role each person might have had in an early city.

government worker	craftworker
town leader	merchant

4 I am skilled at making tools from obsidian. I am very busy, for people in many towns and

cities want to buy my tools. _____

5 My family has ruled the town for many years, and I am now responsible for

governing our community wisely. _____

6 I buy goods from traders and then sell them at the marketplace. _____

7 People come to me to pay their taxes. Some pay in crops and food. Others pay in

goods they make. _____

CALIFORNIA STANDARDS HSS 6.1, 6.1.3, 6.2.2; CS 3, HI 2

Skills: Distinguish Fact from Opinion

DIRECTIONS Read the following excerpts from fictional sources. List two facts and two opinions in the chart that follows each source.

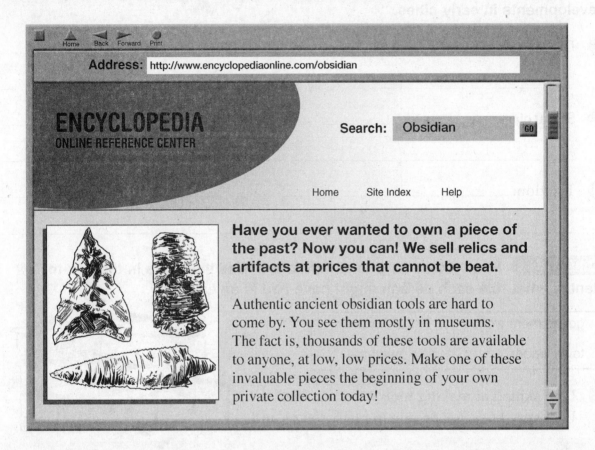

Facts	Opinions
❶ _____	❸ _____
_____	_____
_____	_____
❷ _____	❹ _____
_____	_____
_____	_____

CALIFORNIA STANDARDS HSS 6.1, 6.1.3; HR 2, HI 5   *(continued)*

Name _____ Date _____

Jericho Site Still a Source of Controversy

West Bank, Israel—Archaeologists state that the ancient town of Jericho developed about 7000 B.C.

Today, scientists agree that Jericho was a farming community. However, some disagree on whether irrigation was used in the town. Some believe that there is no question that irrigation must have been used to support large areas of crops. Others think that it is impossible that this early civilization used irrigation.

Facts	Opinions
5 _____ _____ _____ 6 _____ _____ _____	7 _____ _____ _____ _____ 8 _____ _____ _____

Chapter 2

Name _____   Date _____

Study Guide

DIRECTIONS Fill in the missing information in this summary. Use the terms below to complete the report.

Lesson 1	Lesson 2	Lesson 3
10,000	Asia	Jericho
domesticate	plow	government
agricultural revolution	Europe	civilizations
droughts	irrigation	division of labor
8,000	Africa	taxation
climate	barter	social classes

Lesson 1   The end of the Ice Age, about _____ years ago,

brought tremendous changes to the world. For early people in southwestern

Asia, the weather grew warmer and drier, and _____

caused times of food shortages. People learned to adapt to the changing

_____ in new ways.

Farmers in the region experimented with finding seeds that would

produce more successful crops. Experts believe that people in Abu Hureyra

and Jericho were the first to _____ plants and animals.

By _____ years ago, people in regions of Africa,

Asia, and South America had begun to farm in one area, rather than relying

on hunting and gathering in many areas. This time is often referred to as the

_____, because the knowledge of farming that people

developed changed human life dramatically.

CALIFORNIA STANDARDS HSS 6.1.3, 6.2.1, 6.2.2   *(continued)*

Use after reading Chapter 2, pages 48–71.

Lesson 2   Archaeologists have learned a great deal about early farming cultures around the world from the pottery of the Bandkeramik culture in _____, the weaving of cloth in Mehrgarh in _____, and artifacts from villages along the Nile River in _____.

By 6,000 B.C., farmers had developed new technology to improve their way of life. The _____ helped farmers grow larger crops with fewer people, and _____ enabled them to bring water to crops. Surpluses of foods and goods allowed communities to _____ with others to obtain goods they needed. The need for leadership became important in order to control trade and maintain peace.

Lesson 3   Human society continued to grow in complexity. Early towns, such as Çatal Hüyük and _____, were situated along important trade routes and near sources of water, and both established means of protecting themselves.

The success of farming allowed people to do more than just farm. People also became craftworkers, merchants, and traders. This _____ resulted in more changes. _____ began to form as ways of passing on responsibility, power, and leadership. Around 3500 B.C., some towns developed into cities that had specialized workers, marketplaces, public buildings, and an organized system of _____.

In the region of Mesopotamia, early cities such as Kish, Ur, Eridu, and Uruk flourished. _____ was used to pay for many city services, and by 3100 B.C., cities had grown into _____ that covered large regions in Mesopotamia and in Egypt.

READING SOCIAL STUDIES:
MAIN IDEA AND DETAILS

Focus Skill **Early Farmers**

DIRECTIONS Complete this graphic organizer to show that you can identify the main idea and supporting details of how farming and keeping animals changed the way early people lived.

Main Idea and Details

Main Idea

_____

_____

_____

_____

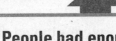

Details

People could now live in permanent settlements.	People had enough surplus to trade with others.	Livestock became a main source of meat.

The Land Between Two Rivers

DIRECTIONS Use your textbook and what you have learned about early Mesopotamia to label the map.

northern Mesopotamia	fertile soil	tributaries
southern Mesopotamia	plateau	Sumer
Tigris River	Taurus Mountains	
Euphrates River	alluvial plain	

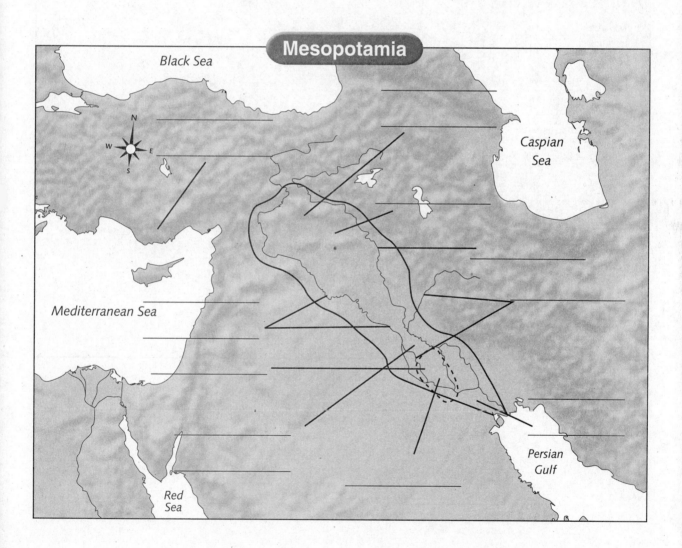

Mesopotamia

Skills: Read a Land Use and Products Map

DIRECTIONS Use the map below to answer the questions on the following page.

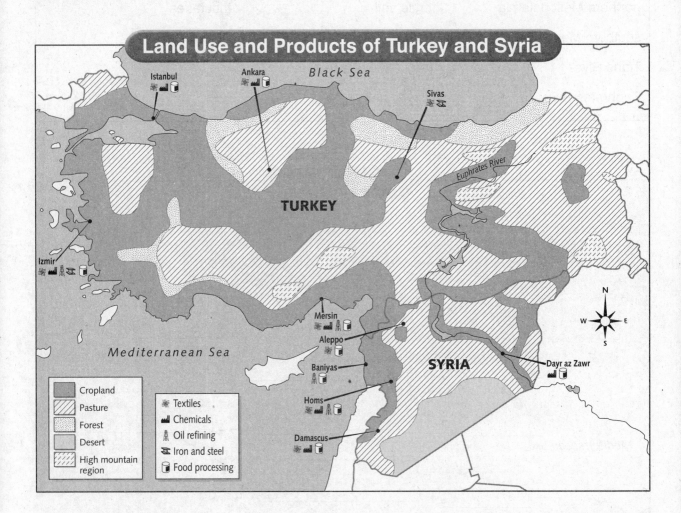

Land Use and Products of Turkey and Syria

Istanbul

Ankara

Black Sea

Sivas

Euphrates River

TURKEY

Izmir

Mediterranean Sea

Mersin

Aleppo

Baniyas

SYRIA

Dayr az Zawr

Homs

Damascus

Cropland
Pasture
Forest
Desert
High mountain region

Textiles
Chemicals
Oil refining
Iron and steel
Food processing

N
W   E
S

CALIFORNIA STANDARDS HSS 6.2; CS 3

(continued)

24 ■ **Homework and Practice Book**   Use after reading Chapter 3, Skill Lesson, pages 100–101.

Name _____ Date _____

1 What is a statement you can make about the land use of the regions near the

Mediterranean Sea? _____

_____

2 Find the southern border region of Syria. What is a statement you can make about

the land use and products of this area? _____

_____

_____

3 Why do you think the land along the Euphrates River is used primarily for

cropland? _____

_____

4 Write a statement that tells how land in Turkey is used in general.

_____

_____

5 Which types of land-use regions are found in Turkey but not in Syria?

_____

6 In which cities will you find oil refineries? _____

_____

7 Write a statement that tells how the products made in Istanbul and Izmir are alike

and how are they different. _____

_____

_____

8 Write a statement that tells how the products made in Damascus and Dayr az

Zawr are alike and different. _____

_____

Independent Sumerian City-States

DIRECTIONS Complete the chart about life in Sumerian city-states. Write a description for the topic named in each section of the chart.

Sumerian City-States	Form of Governing

	Religion

	Trade and Resources

CALIFORNIA STANDARDS HSS 6.2, 6.2.2, 6.2.3; HI 1

26 ■ Homework and Practice Book   Use after reading Chapter 3, Lesson 2, pages 102–107.

Mesopotamian Achievements

DIRECTIONS Complete the chart to tell about the many innovations of the Sumerians.

Sumerian Achievements and Innovations

Farming	Measurements
• developed irrigation	• used quarts to measure weight and volume
• _____	• _____
• _____	• _____
• _____	• _____

Building	Transportation	Writing and Literature
• formed bricks of mud for building homes	• made boats of different materials for various purposes	• wrote down songs and stories
• _____	• _____	• _____
		• _____

CALIFORNIA STANDARDS HSS 6.2, 6.2.2; HI 2

Daily Life in Sumer

DIRECTIONS Write answers to complete the sentences about how people lived in Sumerian city-states.

1 Government officials known as scribes often had great power in Sumerian city-

states because _____

_____

2 Sumerians offered gifts of animals, fruits, and grain to deities because

_____

_____

3 Sumerians who had sold themselves into slavery could

_____

_____

DIRECTIONS Imagine that you are an 11-year-old child in a Sumerian city-state. Write a paragraph to tell about your life. Answer the following questions:

- **What does your family do?**
- **What is your family's social class?**
- **How do you spend your days?**
- **What do you like best about where you live?**

_____

_____

_____

_____

_____

_____

_____

_____

CALIFORNIA STANDARDS HSS 6.2, 6.2.2, 6.2.3; HI 2

The First Empires

DIRECTIONS Complete the time line, using the choices listed below it. Write the number of the event on the space below the correct marker on the time line.

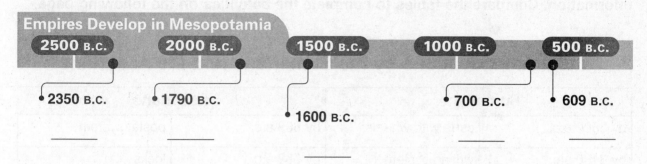

1. The Assyrian Empire rises to become the largest empire in the world at its time

2. Hammurabi conquers the region and forms the Babylonian Empire

3. The Assyrian Empire falls to its enemies and the New Babylonian Empire becomes established

4. The Babylonian Empire is attacked by the Kassites and Hittites and eventually is ruled by the Kassites

5. Sargon gains power and establishes the Akkadian Empire

DIRECTIONS Match the description on the left to the leaders or groups on the right. Write the letter in the space provided.

6. _____ During their rule, they adopted Babylonian laws, religion, and literature.

7. _____ As emperor of the Babylonian Empire, he set up a code of 282 laws to establish clear rules of fairness.

8. _____ The Hanging Gardens of Babylon were constructed during his rule.

9. _____ He maintained rule by choosing loyal officials and keeping a large standing army.

10. _____ During their rule, they developed many innovations, such as building paved roads and establishing a postal system.

a. the Assyrians

b. Nebuchadnezzar

c. the Kassites

d. Sargon

e. Hammurabi

CALIFORNIA STANDARDS HSS 6.2, 6.2.3, 6.2.4; CS 2

Skills: Compare Tables

DIRECTIONS Table A shows one way to classify information about innovations by the Sumerians and the Assyrians. Table B shows another way to present the same information. Compare the tables to complete the activities on the following page.

Table A: Innovations by the Sumerians and the Assyrians

Sumerians		Assyrians	
by 3500 B.C.	carts with wheels	by 609 B.C.	postal system
by 3100 B.C.	writing system	by 609 B.C.	locks
by 2500 B.C.	farming tools made from bronze	by 609 B.C.	magnifying glass
by 2100 B.C.	calendar of 360 days		

Table B: Innovations by the Sumerians and the Assyrians

Innovation	When Developed	By Whom
calendar of 360 days	by 2100 B.C.	Sumerians
carts with wheels	by 3500 B.C.	Sumerians
farming tools made from bronze	by 2500 B.C.	Sumerians
locks	by 609 B.C.	Assyrians
magnifying glass	by 609 B.C.	Assyrians
postal system	by 609 B.C.	Assyrians
writing system	by 3100 B.C.	Sumerians

CALIFORNIA STANDARDS HSS 6.2, 6.2.3; CS 3, HI 2   *(continued)*

30 ▪ **Homework and Practice Book**   Use after reading Chapter 3, Skill Lesson, pages 126–127.

Name _____ Date _____

1 Describe how information is classified, or sorted, in Table A.

_____

_____

_____

2 Describe how information is classified, or sorted, in Table B.

_____

_____

_____

3 Which people invented locks? Tell which table you used to find this information and why.

_____

_____

_____

4 List two important Sumerian innovations. Tell which table you used to find this information and why.

_____

_____

_____

5 Think of another way the same information in the tables could be classified. Write a sentence to describe your idea.

_____

_____

_____

Name _____   Date _____

Study Guide

DIRECTIONS Fill in the missing information in this summary. Use the boxed terms below to help you complete the report.

Lesson 1	Lesson 2	Lesson 3	Lesson 4	Lesson 5
Ubaid	monarchy	ziggurats	social	Assyrian
control	trade	almanacs	deities	Akkadian
Mesopotamia	polytheism	cuneiform	laws	Kassites
irrigation	city-states	quart	craftworkers	Babylonian
	architecture		agriculture	

Lesson 1   Many early civilizations formed in regions with river valleys, because these sources of fresh water were important for survival. The area between the Tigris and Euphrates Rivers became known as _____ or the "land between the rivers." The early people of southern Mesopotomia used _____ , dams, and other methods to help them _____ the rivers. The first known settlements there gave rise to the _____ culture.

Lesson 2   In places such as Ur, Kish, Uruk, and Eridu, _____ formed. Each one was an independent _____ , led by a king who had complete authority. The Sumerians practiced _____ and believed that different gods ruled natural events. Sumerian _____ developed, and the Sumerians constructed temples to their gods. As food surpluses grew and people began to take on work beyond farming, Sumerian cities used _____ to obtain new resources.

CALIFORNIA STANDARDS HSS 6.2, 6.2.1, 6.2.2, 6.2.3, 6.2.4   *(continued)*

Name _____ Date _____

Lesson 3   Sumerians are known for their many innovations. Farmers created

more efficient methods of farming, and used _____ with informa-

tion on planting and irrigation. Standard units of measurement for weight and

volume, such as the _____ , were created by the Sumerians. To honor

their gods, they built temples called _____ in every city. Trade routes

became established. The Sumerians also were the first to develop a system of

writing using _____ symbols.

Lesson 4   The success of _____ allowed Sumerian civilization to

flourish. However, the Sumerians found they needed _____ to keep

order. As fewer people were needed for farming, Sumerians began to special-

ize and became traders, scribes, and _____ . This led to the division

of society into _____ classes. Sumerians also held strong religious

beliefs and worshipped many _____ for protection.

Lesson 5   Around 2350 B.C., Sumer was conquered by an army led by the leader

Sargon. He set up the _____ Empire. The _____ Empire

followed several hundred years later. One of its emperors, Hammurabi, is

remembered for his organized code of laws. After his death, the empire was

controlled by the _____ , who adopted the Babylonian culture. Later,

the _____ Empire gained control of the region. In 609 B.C., however,

the Assyrian Empire fell to its enemies, and the New Babylonian Empire began.

READING SOCIAL STUDIES: SUMMARIZE

 Mesopotamian Achievements

DIRECTIONS Complete this graphic organizer to show that you can summarize the achievements of the Mesopotamians.

Summarize

Key Fact

Improved irrigation and farming tools

➤ **Summary**

_____

_____

_____

_____

Key Fact

Developed a writing system

➤

Key Fact

Used bronze-tipped plows, which made larger fields possible

➤ **Summary**

_____

_____

_____

_____

Key Fact

Used funnels to plant seeds allowing them to grow more crops

➤

The Nile Valley

DIRECTIONS The Nile River was important to the ancient Egyptians for many reasons. Use the terms from the box to complete the graphic organizer about agriculture and religion in ancient Egypt.

afterlife	stored	polytheistic
irrigation	fertile	order
government	natural events	

How the Nile River Influenced the Egyptians

Agriculture

The Nile River provided an important source of water for farming. The river's yearly flooding brought _____ soil, but it was unpredictable. To control the river, the Egyptians built _____ ditches. They also _____ water in ponds and pools. Over time, irrigation and farming were supervised by the _____.

Religious Beliefs

The ancient Egyptians looked for _____ in their world. They created stories to explain _____. They formed a _____ religion, in which specific gods and goddesses controlled specific parts of nature. Because they believed that the sun was reborn each day, Egyptian people believed that they too would have an _____.

DIRECTIONS Write a short paragraph that tells how the Nile River also influenced trade, travel, and shipbuilding in ancient Egypt.

_____

_____

_____

_____

CALIFORNIA STANDARDS HSS 6.2, 6.2.1, 6.2.2, 6.2.3, 6.2.6; HI 1, 2, 3

Skills: Compare Map Projections

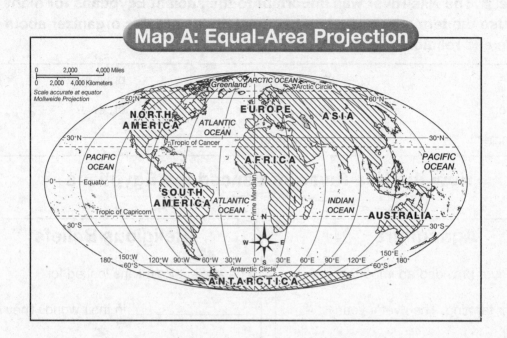

Map A: Equal-Area Projection

0   2,000   4,000 Miles
0   2,000   4,000 Kilometers
Scale accurate at equator
Mollweide Projection

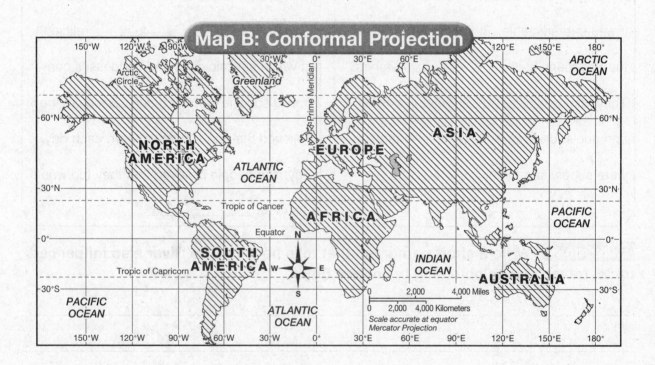

Map B: Conformal Projection

0   2,000   4,000 Miles
0   2,000   4,000 Kilometers
Scale accurate at equator
Mercator Projection

🐻 **CALIFORNIA STANDARDS HSS 6.2; CS 3**   *(continued)*

36 ▪ **Homework and Practice Book**   Use after reading Chapter 4, Skill Lesson, pages 140–141.

Name _____ Date _____

An equal-area projection map shows the correct size of regions in relation to each other, but distorts their shapes. A conformal projection map distorts the size of regions, especially near the poles, but shows shapes and directions correctly. Use the maps on page 36 to complete the activities below.

1 Which projection shows the correct size of Australia in relation to Africa?

_____

2 Which projection would you use to study the shape of South America?

_____

3 Which projection would you use to determine the actual direction from Asia to Australia?

_____

4 What happens to lines of latitude on Map B, the conformal projection map?

_____

_____

_____

5 Why is it important to identify the type of projection a map uses?

_____

_____

_____

The Old Kingdom

DIRECTIONS The unification of Egypt by King Narmer in about 3100 B.C. was a significant event for many reasons. Complete the statements below that tell about the importance of this event. Include ideas about unifying people, religion, and government in your responses.

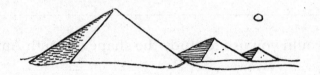

▲ Before Egypt was unified under King Narmer, the region was made up of

_____

▲ When King Narmer unified Egypt, he formed the world's first nation-state, which is

_____

_____

▲ King Narmer established the world's first dynasty, which is

_____

_____

▲ Kings of the Old Kingdom were seen as living gods, which meant that

_____

_____

▲ The great pyramids were an important part of Egyptian culture because

_____

_____

CALIFORNIA STANDARDS HSS 6.2, 6.2.3, 6.2.5; HI 2, 3   *(continued)*

Name _____ Date _____

reeds	hieroglyphs	scrolls
stone	papyrus	

About 3100 B.C., the Egyptians developed a form of writing using

_____ . At first, they carved on _____ for

religious purposes. Later, to record other kinds of information, the

Egyptians created a paperlike material called _____

by pressing together layers of plant stalks. Scribes wrote using

sharpened _____ and formed long _____

on which they recorded the history of their nation.

DIRECTIONS Answer the questions below about how ancient Egyptians prepared for the afterlife.

1 Why did Egyptians preserve the bodies of the dead? _____

_____

2 What items were placed in the tomb with a royal mummy? _____

_____

_____

3 What is the *Book of the Dead*? _____

_____

4 What was the importance of the ceremony in the afterlife that is called the

"weighing of the heart"? _____

_____

The Middle Kingdom

DIRECTIONS Use the terms from the box to complete the paragraph about the Middle Kingdom in Egypt.

stable	Lower Egypt	northern Nubia	famine	weakened

By the end of the Old Kingdom, Egypt faced civil war, drought, and widespread

_____. The kingdom was reunited in about 2040 B.C., and remained

_____ for about 250 years. Amenemhet ruled during Dynasty 12. He

conquered _____ and brought security to the kingdom. Other rul-

ers in Dynasty 12 built upon his achievements and directed huge building projects.

During Dynasty 13, however, Egypt was _____. The Hyksos conquered

_____ by 1640 B.C., and brought cultural changes to Egypt.

DIRECTIONS Trade expanded greatly in Egypt during Dynasty 12. Complete the chart about trade during this time.

To what places did traders travel?	What resources were brought to Egypt?
_____ _____ _____	_____ _____ _____
What was trade over land like?	**What was sea trade like?**
_____ _____ _____	_____ _____ _____
Why did Egypt need certain resources from trade, such as copper and wood?	
_____	

CALIFORNIA STANDARDS HSS 6.2, 6.2.6; HI 1, 2

40 ▪ Homework and Practice Book   Use after reading Chapter 4, Lesson 3, pages 150–154.

Skills: Distinguish Importance of Information

DIRECTIONS Read the following passage about the Egyptian pharaoh Ramses II. As you read, try to identify the importance of statements and ideas. Then answer the questions that follow.

You Will Remember His Name

Ramses II, also known as Ramses the Great, ruled Egypt as pharaoh from about 1280 B.C. to 1224 B.C. He began numerous immense construction projects during his reign, including great temples at Karnak, Luxor, and Abu Simbel.

Some historians believe that Ramses II must have been very proud of himself, because he had many monuments and statues constructed in his own honor. He even directed the construction of his own tomb at Thebes just after he began his reign.

Ramses II probably was not a humble ruler. He enjoyed wearing the gold and lapis lazuli adornments made for him as pharaoh. He may have been extremely vain about his appearance.

Some say that Ramses II was preoccupied with making himself a legend. Many stories tell of his great courage and bravery in battle. Whether these stories are true or not, Ramses II did defend Egypt and made the kingdom prosperous. He was certainly remembered, as nine other pharaohs took the name Ramses in his honor.

1 Is the sentence "He even directed the construction of his own tomb at Thebes just after he began his reign" relevant or irrelevant? Explain your response.

_____

_____

2 Is the statement "He enjoyed wearing the gold and lapis lazuli adornments made for him as pharaoh" essential or incidental information? Explain your response.

_____

_____

3 Is the statement "Ramses II did defend Egypt and made the Kingdom prosperous" verifiable or unverifiable? Explain your response.

_____

_____

_____

 CALIFORNIA STANDARDS HSS 6.2.7; HR 3, HI 2

Name _____ Date _____

The New Kingdom

DIRECTIONS Read the statements about leaders of Egypt during the New Kingdom. Chose the correct leader's name from the box and write it in the space next to each statement. You may use some names more than once.

Thutmose III	Tutankhaton
Ramses II	Nefertiti
Hatshepsut	Amenhotep IV

1 _____ This young ruler was pharaoh from the time he was nine until he died at the age of eighteen. During his reign, he changed his name to Tutankhamen, and the old gods were restored.

2 _____ In the later years of his reign, this leader directed the construction of grand temples in all parts of Egypt.

3 _____ As pharaoh, she sent a trading expedition to the Red Sea, and it returned with goods such as ebony and gold.

4 _____ This leader brought great change to Egypt through his religious beliefs. He worshipped just one god, and even changed his own name to Akhenaton.

5 _____ Under the rule of this leader, Egypt grew to its greatest size. He was the stepson of Hatshepsut.

6 _____ This ruler's new name meant "Living Image of Amon."

7 _____ This ruler was one of the few women to rule Egypt. She ordered that conquered lands pay tribute to Egypt in exchange for protection.

8 _____ This pharaoh brought prosperity to Egypt in his long reign. He continually defended Egypt and strengthened the kingdom.

9 _____ Along with her husband the pharaoh, she believed deeply in just one god, Aton, the god of the sun.

10 _____ This ruler removed all names of all gods but one from temples and tombs. He moved Egypt's capital to a new city, Akhetaten.

CALIFORNIA STANDARDS HSS 6.2, 6.2.3, 6.2.5, 6.2.7; HI 6 *(continued)*

42 ▪ Homework and Practice Book Use after reading Chapter 4, Lesson 4, pages 158–163.

Name _____ Date _____

DIRECTIONS Complete the diagram to show how society was structured
in ancient Egypt. On the lines provided, describe who belonged to each level
of society.

Structure of Egyptian Society

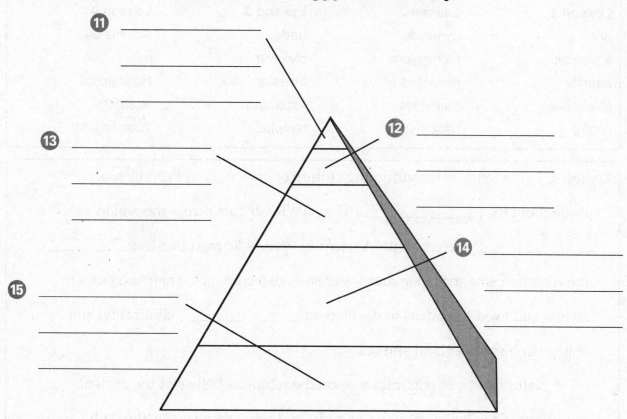

11 _____

_____

_____

13 _____

_____

12 _____

_____

_____

14 _____

_____

15 _____

_____

_____

DIRECTIONS Read the following statements about the art and architecture of
the New Kingdom. Write *T* next to each statement that is true and *F* next to each
statement that is false.

16 _____ Pyramids were commonly constructed during the New Kingdom.

17 _____ Houses of the New Kingdom often had separate levels for business and for
living space.

18 _____ We know that music was important to the Egyptians because tomb paintings
show people dancing and playing instruments.

19 _____ Temples of the New Kingdom were very different from each other, with
separate designs and plans.

20 _____ Most buildings of the New Kingdom were made from mud bricks.

Use after reading Chapter 4, Lesson 4, pages 158–163.   **Homework and Practice Book ▪ 43**

Study Guide

DIRECTIONS Fill in the missing information in this article. Use the terms below to help you complete the article.

Lesson 1	Lesson 2	Lesson 3	Lesson 4
arid	pyramids	trade	Akhenaton
advanced	hieroglyphs	civil war	reign
afterlife	dynasties	invasion	Hatshepsut
Nile Valley	mummies	expansion	pharaohs
control	nation-state	temples	Tutankhamen

Lesson 1   Evidence of the intriguing culture of ancient Egypt can be found throughout the _____. The Nile River cuts across the region's _____ desert lands. Ancient Egyptians learned to _____ the river by using irrigation and water storage techniques. Their successes in farming allowed Egyptians to develop an _____ civilization and engage in trade over land and sea.

Nature had a strong influence on the religious beliefs of the ancient Egyptians. They believed in many gods, and what they saw as the daily rebirth of the sun led to their belief in an _____.

Lesson 2   About 3100 B.C., King Narmer united Upper and Lower Egypt to create the world's first _____ and begin a period known as the Old Kingdom. Series of rulers from the same families, called _____, led Egypt for the next 3,000 years.

During the time of the Old Kingdom, immense _____ were constructed and served as places for burial for Egyptian rulers. Bodies were preserved as _____ and placed in tombs with everything they

CALIFORNIA STANDARDS HSS 6.2.1, 6.2.2, 6.2.3, 6.2.5, 6.2.6   *(continued)*

44 ▪ Homework and Practice Book   Use after reading Chapter 4, pages 134–163.

Lesson 2 *(continued)*   would need in their next life.

During this time, the Egyptians developed a form of writing known as

_____. First used for religious purposes, writing was used later

for keeping records.

Lesson 3   By the end of the Old Kingdom, _____, drought, and

famine had split Egypt. In 2040 B.C., it was reunited again. This period, which

lasted until 1786 B.C., is known as the Middle Kingdom.

The Middle Kingdom was a time of great _____ in many

ways. Large-scale building projects took place to strengthen farming and the

nation's security. Great _____ were constructed to honor the dead.

_____ developed rapidly to bring needed resources to Egypt.

By the end of the Middle Kingdom, Egypt faced _____

from neighboring regions. By about 1640 B.C., the Hyksos gained control of

Lower Egypt.

Lesson 4   The rule of Dynasty 18 marks the beginning of the New Kingdom.

During this time, rulers came to be known as _____. The Egyptian

Empire expanded greatly under leaders such as _____ and her

stepson Thutmose III.

The reign of _____ brought great religious conflict, as

he believed in just one god. Under the short rule of the young ruler

_____, the old gods were restored.

Ramses II ruled Egypt for 65 years. His _____ expanded the

empire and brought great prosperity.

Name _____ Date _____

READING SOCIAL STUDIES: SUMMARIZE

(Focus Skill) Early Egyptian Civilization

DIRECTIONS Complete this graphic organizer to show that you can summarize how geography affected the Egyptian civilization.

Summarize

Key Fact

Egypt's political structure was affected by geography.

➤

Summary

_____
_____
_____

Key Fact

The economic structure of early Egypt was affected by geography.

➤

_____
_____

Key Fact

The Egyptians built irrigation ditches to bring water from the Nile to the fields.

➤

Summary

_____
_____
_____

Key Fact

The Egyptians built dams and dikes to control yearly flooding.

➤

_____
_____

 CALIFORNIA STANDARDS HSS 6.2, 6.2.1, 6.2.2

Use after reading Chapter 4, pages 134–163.

The Land Called Nubia

DIRECTIONS Complete the table to show how the lands and people of ancient Egypt and Nubia were alike and how they were different.

	Egypt	Nubia
Landforms	wide plains along the Nile River	_____ _____ _____
The Nile River	smooth-flowing river	_____ _____ _____
Impact of Climate	very little rain; the Nile was the main source of water	_____ _____ _____
How People Lived	people were primarily farmers	_____ _____ _____

CALIFORNIA STANDARDS HSS 6.2, 6.2.1, 6.2.2, 6.2.8; CS 2, HI 2

(continued)

Name _____ Date _____

DIRECTIONS Use the terms from the box to complete the passage about how the Nubians developed trade.

commercial	imported	economy	exported

The Nubians _____ goods such as leopard skins, ebony, ivory, and spices from

the south. They then _____ these goods to the north. These activities allowed

Nubia to create _____ relations with Egypt. As Nubia's trade flourished, so did

Nubia's _____ .

DIRECTIONS Complete the time line about the development and control of Nubia using the choices listed below the time line. Write the letter of the event in the space below the correct marker on the time line.

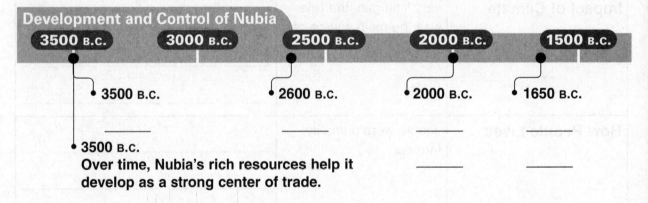

Development and Control of Nubia

3500 B.C.   3000 B.C.   2500 B.C.   2000 B.C.   1500 B.C.

3500 B.C.   2600 B.C.   2000 B.C.   1650 B.C.

_____   _____   _____

3500 B.C.
Over time, Nubia's rich resources help it
develop as a strong center of trade.   _____   _____

A. The Kushite capital, Kerma, grows wealthy as it develops as a center of trade.

B. Northern Nubia is annexed by Egypt.

C. Nubian communities based on herding form along the Nile River.

D. The kingdom of Kush forms in southern Nubia.

E. Egypt takes control of trade routes in northern Nubia.

F. The Kushites force the Egyptians out of Nubia and regain their independence.

New Kingdoms of Kush

DIRECTIONS Number the sentences according
to the order in which the events occurred.

_____ King Kashta's son Piye conquers
Lower Egypt, and all of Egypt is
under Kushite control.

_____ Egypt is invaded by the
Assyrians, and the Kushites
retreat to Napata.

_____ The pharaoh Taharqa rules
the Kushite dynasty and
directs many building
projects, including
temples.

_____ The Kushites build a
new capital city, called
Napata, where they are
free from Egyptian rule.

_____ The Kushites establish a new capital city, called Meroë, near the sixth cataract
of the Nile River.

_____ The Kushites are defeated by the Axumites, and by the end of the fourth century
A.D., the Kushite civilization had fallen.

_____ Piye's brother Shabaka rules as pharaoh, beginning Dynasty 25 in Egypt.

_____ In 750 B.C., Upper Egypt is captured by the Kushites, led by King Kashta.

_____ Napata is attacked by the Assyrians after Taharqa's death.

_____ Meroë's importance as a trading center is weakened over time, and the
Axumites begin to attack Kushite towns.

| CALIFORNIA STANDARDS HSS 6.2, 6.2.1, 6.2.2, 6.2.8; CS 1, HI 1 |

(continued)

Name _____ Date _____

Answer the questions about Kush that follow.

1 How did Pharaoh Taharqa and other Kushite pharaohs of Dynasty 25 help bring back the glory of Egypt?

_____

_____

2 How did the Kushites lose control of Egypt to the Assyrians?

_____

_____

_____

3 Why was Meroë important? How did it lose its importance?

_____

_____

_____

_____

4 What role did women play in ruling Meroë?

_____

_____

_____

5 Why did the Nubians create a written language? What do historians know about the written form of this language?

_____

_____

_____

_____

Use after reading Chapter 5, Lesson 2, pages 178–182.

Skills: Solve a Problem

DIRECTIONS The people of the Kushite civilization faced challenges that were similar to some of those faced by the ancient Egyptians. One common challenge was the lack of rainfall. Read about one way the Kushites found to conserve water and use it for irrigation and farming. Then complete the activities on the next page.

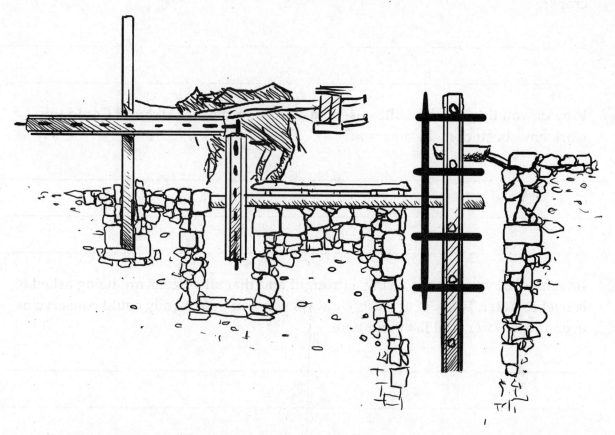

The *saqia* was a type of water wheel that may have first been used in Mesopotamia. The Kushites used it in lower Nubia near the second cataract of the Nile River. A large animal, such as an ox, was used to turn a large wheel, which was parallel to the ground. When this wheel moved, it made a second wheel revolve. This wheel was connected to a third wheel, which was set within a well containing water. Pots were set along this wheel and would fill with water as the wheel revolved. When a pot reached the top of the wheel, it would tip and spill into a trough, which was connected to irrigation canals.

The *saqia* helped the Kushites conserve rainwater and move it to another area. Like the Egyptians, the Kushites also conserved water by creating pools and lakes for large water storage areas, and made vessels of many sizes to hold and carry water.

CALIFORNIA STANDARDS HSS 6.2, 6.2.2

(continued)

Name _____ Date _____

1 How did the *saqia* help the Kushites solve the problem of conserving water?

_____

_____

2 How did the *saqia* help the Kushites solve the problem of getting water to their crops?

_____

_____

3 Why do you think the Kushites used an ox to turn the large wheel? Could this work have been done by a person?

_____

_____

_____

4 Imagine that your area is facing a drought and that all citizens are being asked to conserve water. Think of at least five ways you and your family could conserve or even reuse water, and list them here.

_____

_____

_____

_____

5 Decide which two of your ideas would be the best for conserving water. Why would you use these ideas?

_____

_____

_____

_____

Chapter 5

Name _____   Date _____

Study Guide

DIRECTIONS Fill in the missing information in this biographical account. Use the terms below to help you complete the account.

Lesson 1		Lesson 2	
export	cataracts	Piye	Red Sea
annexed	import	Taharqa	Amani-Shakete
herding	resources	Axum	Napata
allies	independence	Kashta	

My father is a merchant here in our Kushite city of Meroë. He is very worried about our future. As I learn more about our history from him, I grow more worried, too.

Lesson 1   My father says that our people long ago built a strong relationship

with Egypt. Our land along the Nile River was very different from Egypt's.

Travel along the boulders and rapids of the river's _____ was very

difficult. Our land was better suited for _____ than for farming.

But our land was rich in many _____ that the Egyptians

wanted, especially gold, copper, and stone. Our people could also

_____ goods from the south and _____ them to

the north. The Egyptians eventually controlled our lands, but our people

fought back and regained our _____. Our powerful kings

helped make our lands prosperous and became _____ of the

Hyksos, who controlled much of Egypt.

However, the Egyptians fought for and regained their lands from the

Hyksos. Soon, our lands were _____ again by Egypt. Many of our

people took on Egyptian ways and customs.

Lesson 2   My father tells me that our people grew stronger as the Egyptians grew weaker. We built a new capital city, called _____, farther south along the Nile, where we were free from Egyptian rule. We formed our own Kushite dynasty, and in time, our leader, King _____, conquered Upper Egypt. His son _____ captured Lower Egypt. Because of this, the Kushites controlled Egypt for many years.

During this time of our rule, called Dynasty 25, our pharaohs accomplished many great things. The great _____ built many great temples. Our rule brought back Egypt's glory. However, the people known as the Assyrians later conquered Egypt, and our Kushite rule of that land came to an end.

Our leaders built our city here at Meroë. We made it a center of trade, and rebuilt our power. Many of our strong rulers have been women, such as Queen _____. We have our own written language, and we keep records of our lives. We take great pride in our ways and our people, and we have been rich and prosperous.

However, our times are now troubled. The Greek rulers have set up ports on the _____, and overland trade has decreased greatly. My father says the king of _____ wants to attack our lands. My father's fears are now my fears. What will become of us?

READING SOCIAL STUDIES: SUMMARIZE

⭐ **Focus Skill** **Kushite Rule of Egypt**

DIRECTIONS Complete this graphic organizer to show that you can **summarize** Kushite rule of Egypt.

Summarize

Key Fact

In 750 B.C., a Kushite king conquered Upper Egypt.

➤

Summary
_____
_____
_____
_____

Key Fact

Later, his son Piye conquered Lower Egypt.

➤

Key Fact

As trade developed, the people of Meroë needed to keep trade records.

➤

Summary
_____
_____
_____
_____

Key Fact

The people of Meroë created the first Nubian written language.

➤

🐻 **CALIFORNIA STANDARDS HSS 6.2, 6.2.6, 6.2.8**

Beginnings of the Hebrew People

DIRECTIONS Each statement tells about a person from early Jewish history. Identify who is described, and write the number of the statement in the chart below the person's name.

1 He was the father of Jacob.

2 In hopes of saving him, his mother set him afloat in a basket on the Nile.

3 He was reunited with his 11 brothers after a long separation.

4 He was a son of Jacob.

5 He made a covenant to worship God alone and left Mesopotamia with his family to settle in Canaan.

6 He was a son of Abraham.

7 He became known as the father of the Jewish people.

8 His brothers became jealous of him and sold him to traders.

9 He was raised as an Egyptian, but knew that he was an Israelite.

10 Each of his 12 sons later led the tribes known as Israelites.

11 He was born in Mesopotamia in about 2000 B.C.

12 He was given the Ten Commandments by God.

13 He became a trusted adviser to the pharaoh.

14 He also became known as Israel.

15 He was told by God to demand freedom for the Israelites.

Abraham
___
___
Isaac
___
___
Jacob
___
___
Joseph
___
___
___
Moses
___
___
___

CALIFORNIA STANDARDS HSS 6.3, 6.3.1, 6.3.2, 6.3.3, 6.3.4

(continued)

Use after reading Chapter 6, Lesson 1, pages 204–208.

Name _____ Date _____

16 The ancient Hebrews practiced monotheism, or belief in one God. How was this
different from the religious beliefs of other people during that time?

_____

_____

17 What are the sources of information about the ancient Hebrews? By whom are
they used today?

_____

_____

_____

_____

18 Describe the route and the events of the Exodus.

_____

_____

_____

_____

19 What is the importance of the Ten Commandments? How are they still important
today?

_____

_____

_____

The Kingdom of Israel

DIRECTIONS Write a short summary that tells what each of the following leaders did for the Israelites.

Samuel: _____

_____

_____

Saul: _____

_____

_____

David: _____

_____

_____

DIRECTIONS Read through the following list of Solomon's achievements during his rule. Choose one of these achievements and explain how it contributed to bringing peace and stability to the kingdom.

King Solomon's Achievements	
• directed the building of the temple at Jerusalem	• built a large army and made alliances with neighboring regions
• divided kingdom into 12 tax districts with separate leaders and services	• authored many proverbs that show a truth about life
• made trade agreements with other regions	

Achievement: _____

_____

_____

CALIFORNIA STANDARDS HSS 6.3, 6.3.3, 6.3.4; HI 2

Name _____ Date _____

Skills: Make an Economic Choice

DIRECTIONS Read this fictional passage about a farmer in the kingdom of Israel and the economic choices he faces. Then complete the activities on the following page.

I come from a family that has farmed the land for generations. When I was very young, my father taught me how to prepare the soil, plant seeds, and harvest crops. Now I am grown and have a family. My wife and I have a young boy and will soon have another child.

My wife and I have been talking about our lives. I have told her that I do not enjoy farming. It can be hard and difficult, and I do not think that I am an especially good farmer, even though my father has taught me well. While I do not care for great wealth, I bring in very little money. My wife sometimes cares for the small children of some wealthy people, and this helps our finances, but I know it can be hard for her. What I want most of all is to give my family a better life.

My uncle is a carpenter. He, too, works long hours at a job that is sometimes difficult, but his income is greater than ours. He has offered me a position as an apprentice under him, and he would teach me how to be a carpenter. While I have little experience, I think I would be much happier as a carpenter, and my wife would not need to find extra work to help us.

I have other things to consider, too. I have watched my uncle at work, and he can be a harsh supervisor. He demands much of his workers, and he sometimes treats them unkindly. I am concerned about this. I am also concerned that I do not want to show disrespect to my father by becoming a carpenter and leaving farming behind.

My wife tells me that she will support the choice I make, whichever it may be. I am grateful to her, but I would like to make her life easier. I know that my father would probably not be happy if I decided to become a carpenter, but I also know that he is kind and understanding.

 CALIFORNIA STANDARDS HSS 6.3, HI 2, 3, 6

(continued)

Name _____ Date _____

1 What economic choice does this young farmer face?

_____

_____

_____

2 What will be his opportunity cost if he decides to continue farming?

_____

_____

_____

3 What trade-offs will he face if he decides to become a carpenter?

_____

_____

4 Why is making more money important to this young farmer?

_____

_____

_____

5 Imagine that you are a close friend of this young farmer. What choice do you think he should make? Write the advice you would give to your friend.

_____

_____

_____

_____

_____

Changes for Israel

DIRECTIONS The chart below shows events that brought great changes to the kingdom of Israel. Complete the chart by describing the outcomes of the events.

Events	Outcomes
King Rehoboam promises to rule the northern tribes of Israel more harshly than in the past. ➡	
Assyria invades and conquers Israel. ➡	
Led by Hezekiah, the Judaeans successfully fight off invasion by the Assyrians. ➡	

DIRECTIONS Answer the question about Jewish culture.

1 When the Assyrians invaded, many Israelites were forced into exile. What effect did this have on the Israelite culture? _____

_____

_____

CALIFORNIA STANDARDS HSS 6.3, 6.3.2, 6.3.4, 6.3.5; HI 2, 3

Skills: Make a Thoughtful Decision

DIRECTIONS Decisions can have far-reaching consequences. Read the passages to review the decision Rehoboam made, and answer the questions.

The northern tribes of Israel had been unhappy under Solomon, and felt that they had received unfair treatment from him. They had been forced to work on building projects and pay taxes to support the projects, while the southern tribes had been free of these demands.

When Rehoboam became king of Israel after the death of his father, the northern tribes demanded that he put an end to the burdens that had been placed upon them by Solomon.

1 Rehoboam had to make a decision. What do you think was his main goal?

_____

_____

2 What were two choices Rehoboam could have made?

_____

3 What might have been the possible consequences of each choice?

_____

_____

Rehoboam decided to ignore the demands of the northern tribes, and further vowed to make their burdens heavier. This decision resulted in a split in the kingdom of Israel. The northern tribes rebelled and formed their own kingdom. The two kingdoms were in conflict for the next 200 years.

4 Why do you think Rehoboam decided to refuse the demands of the northern

tribes? _____

_____

5 What were the long-term effects of Rehoboam's decision on Jewish history and

culture? _____

_____

CALIFORNIA STANDARDS HSS 6.3, 6.3.4; HI 1, 2, 3, 4 *(continued)*

Name _____ Date _____

DIRECTIONS When the Assyrians captured Israel, many Israelites were forced from their lands. The Assyrians settled in Samaria, and mixed with the Israelites who were allowed to stay. Imagine that an Israelite metalworker living in Samaria with the Assyrians wants to decide whether to stay in Samaria or leave to find other Israelites who may be starting new lives in other places. Complete the chart about the metalworker's choices.

What is one choice?	What is another choice?
_____ _____ _____	_____ _____ _____

↓ ↓

What are the possible consequences of this choice?	What are the possible consequences of this choice?
_____ _____ _____ _____	_____ _____ _____ _____

↓ ↓

What choice do you think will have the best consequences? Why?

_____

_____

_____

_____

Chapter 6

Name _____   Date _____

Study Guide

DIRECTIONS Fill in the missing information in this summary. Use the terms below to help you complete the summary.

Lesson 1	Lesson 2	Lesson 3
Mount Sinai	Saul	Assyria
Exodus	proverbs	northern
Mesopotamia	tribes	Hezekiah
Moses	Samuel	Samaria
monotheism	David	Rehoboam
covenant	territories	southern
	Jerusalem	

Lesson 1   The roots of the Jewish religion reach back thousands of years.

Historians believe that Abraham was born in the 1900s B.C. During this time in

_____, people believed in many gods. According to the Hebrew

Bible, God spoke to Abraham and told him to leave and settle with his family

in Canaan. Once there, God made a _____ with Abraham. God

promised that Canaan would belong to Abraham and his descendants as long

as Abraham agreed to worship God alone. Abraham's beliefs brought a new

religious concept, called _____, to the world.

   The Hebrew Bible states that the ancient Hebrews, later called Israelites,

became slaves in Egypt. The Israelites, led by _____, fled from

Egypt in what is called the _____. The Israelites traveled for

many years, and at _____, they received the Ten Commandments.

This set of laws for responsible living has influenced many religions and ways of

thinking.

CALIFORNIA STANDARDS HSS 6.3, 6.3.1, 6.3.2, 6.3.3, 6.3.4   *(continued)*

Name _____ Date _____

Lesson 2   The Hebrew Bible says that the Israelites settled in Canaan, but they

faced invasion from neighboring kingdoms. They asked _____,

a trusted judge, to appoint a king for them. He chose _____

to lead them. Under his rule, the kingdom of Israel conquered new

_____.

Israel's next king, _____, expanded the kingdom of Israel,

even defeating the Philistines. He chose a new capital city, _____,

that belonged to all of the _____ of Israel. Following his father's

rule, King Solomon directed many building projects, and planned a temple for

the capital city. Solomon was particularly known for his _____, or

short sayings that express a truth about life.

Lesson 3   Under the rule of King _____, the kingdom of Israel

split into two parts. The tribes in the _____ lands revolted and

formed their own kingdom of Israel. _____ became their capital

city. The lands of the _____ tribes became known as Judah. Their

capital, Jerusalem, remained a holy place.

Israel was surrounded by powerful enemies who wanted Israel's land. Israel

was invaded and captured by _____, and many Israelites were

forced to leave their land. The kingdom of Judah, led by _____,

successfully fought off the Assyrians, and Judaism survived.

READING SOCIAL STUDIES: GENERALIZE

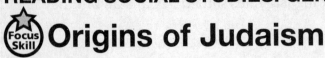

Origins of Judaism

DIRECTIONS Complete this graphic organizer to make a generalization about the development of the ancient Hebrews' religion.

Generalize

Facts

Judaism is based on monotheism.	The Ten Commandments became an important part.	The Israelites formed a kingdom.	King Solomon built a temple in Jerusalem.

Generalization

_____

_____

_____

_____

_____

_____

CALIFORNIA STANDARDS HSS 6.3, 6.3.1, 6.3.2, 6.3.4

Name _____   Date _____

Defeat and New Beginnings

DIRECTIONS Complete the chart to show how Jewish culture was strengthened or weakened by events and ideas after 597 B.C. Then answer the question that follows.

Events and Ideas	Did this strengthen or weaken Jewish culture? How?
The Babylonian Exile	This weakened Jewish culture. The Jews' Temple was destroyed, and they were forced to leave their land.
The teachings of Jeremiah	
As part of the Persian Empire, under Cyrus	
The Jewish Diaspora	

Tell how synagogues came to be formed and describe their purposes.

_____

_____

_____

CALIFORNIA STANDARDS HSS 6.3, 6.3.2, 6.3.4, 6.3.5

Skills: Use a Cultural Map

DIRECTIONS Read about the map that shows where some major religions are practiced today. Then use the map to complete the activities on the following page.

The map below shows where some major religions are practiced today in parts of Africa, Europe, and Asia. Roman Catholic, Protestant, and Eastern Orthodox are all branches of Christianity. Sunni Muslim and Shiite Muslim are two branches of Islam.

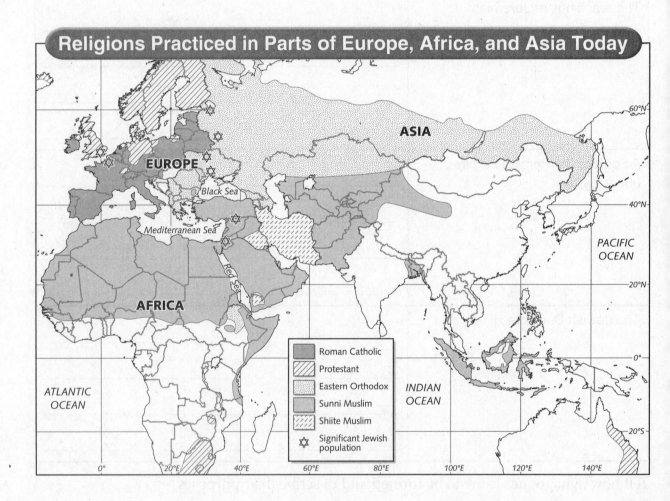

Religions Practiced in Parts of Europe, Africa, and Asia Today

CALIFORNIA STANDARDS HSS 6.3, 6.3.2, 6.3.5; CS 3

(continued)

68 ▪ **Homework and Practice Book**   Use after reading Chapter 7, Skill Lesson, pages 240–241.

Name _____ Date _____

1 Write a summary of where Islam, Christianity, and Judaism are practiced today in the area of the world shown on the map.

_____

_____

_____

_____

2 How are the branches of Islam practiced in the parts of Africa included on the map different from those practiced in southwestern Asia?

_____

_____

_____

3 Summarize where the different branches of Christianity are practiced in the parts of Europe shown on the map.

_____

_____

4 Based on the map, compare the presence of Judaism to that of the other religions shown.

_____

_____

5 Using the map, what conclusion can you draw about where the Jewish people live in parts of Europe and Asia today?

_____

_____

_____

Continuing Traditions

DIRECTIONS Complete the sequence chart by filling in the missing information. Use the terms from the box to help you complete the chart.

167 B.C.	A.D. 70	A.D. 132	200 B.C.	Judah Maccabee
Greek	Romans	Alexander the Great	Bar Kokhba	Yohanan ben Zaccai

332 B.C.: Judaea is conquered by _____, who allows the Jews to continue their religious worship.

⬇

_____ : Under a new ruler, all Judaeans are forced to worship _____ gods.

⬇

_____ : Led by _____, the Jewish people revolt. They recapture Jerusalem, and worship at the Temple is restored.

⬇

63 B.C.: Judaea is overtaken by the _____ . Under their rule, Judaism is disrespected. Treated poorly, the Jewish people rebel.

⬇

_____ : Jerusalem is attacked by the Romans. The city and the Temple are destroyed. Later, _____ establishes a school and center of learning for Jewish culture.

⬇

_____ : Led by _____ , the Jewish people revolt against Roman rule. They are defeated, and nearly all Jews are sent into exile.

CALIFORNIA STANDARDS HSS 6.3, 6.3.2, 6.3.3, 6.3.4, 6.3.5; HI 3   *(continued)*

Name _____ Date _____

| the Torah | the Nevi'im | the Ketuvim | the Commentaries |

1 Which part of the Hebrew Bible includes the account of Ruth and Naomi?

_____

2 In which part of the Hebrew Bible would you find the account of Noah?

_____

3 What writings help explain questions about

Jewish law? _____

4 Which part of the Hebrew Bible includes the teachings of prophets such as

Jeremiah? _____

5 In which part of the Hebrew Bible can the Ten Commandments be found?

_____

6 In which part of the Hebrew Bible can you find the histories of Israelite kings?

_____

7 What important similarity do Judaism, Christianity, and Islam have?

_____

_____

Study Guide

DIRECTIONS Fill in the missing information in this article. Use the boxed terms below to help you complete the article.

Lesson 1		Lesson 2	
Ezra	Jeremiah	Nevi'im	Yohanan ben Zaccai
rabbis	Exile	Romans	Torah
Cyrus	theocracy	Judah Maccabee	
scattered	canonized	Ketuvim	
synagogues		Greeks	

Lesson 1   In 586 B.C., the Babylonians destroyed Jerusalem and the citizens of Judah were forced to leave their homeland to live in Babylon. This event is known as the Babylonian _____. The prophet _____ brought hope to the Jews by telling them that they could worship God everywhere.

The exiled people of Judah established community centers, later called _____, in Babylon. Teachers called _____ taught the Jews about their history and traditions. These changes helped Judaism continue and develop.

In 538 B.C., Babylon was conquered by the Persians. The Persian leader _____ allowed the Jews to reclaim the land of Judah and rebuild their Temple. However, the Jewish Diaspora continued, with many Jews remaining _____ outside of Judah.

The Jewish leader _____ brought many Jews back to Jerusalem. He also helped restore Judaism by focusing attention on the Torah.

CALIFORNIA STANDARDS HSS 6.3, 6.3.1, 6.3.2, 6.3.3, 6.3.4, 6.3.5   *(continued)*

Lesson 1 (*continued*) Governed as a _____, Judah depended on the Torah as a source of religious laws. The Torah was later _____ as an official part of Judaism.

Lesson 2 The Judaeans faced still more challenges. Their land was conquered by Alexander the Great in 332 B.C., and by 200 B.C., all Judaeans were forced to worship the gods of the _____. However, a strong Jewish leader, _____, led a revolt in 167 B.C. The Jews regained all of Judaea in this struggle and restored worship at their Temple.

By 63 B.C., Judaea was controlled by the Roman Empire. The Jewish people suffered greatly under Roman rule. In A.D. 70, Jerusalem and the Temple were destroyed by the _____.

The actions of the rabbi _____ helped Judaism endure. He established a Jewish school, which grew into a center of Jewish life.

The Hebrew Bible is seen as both history and literature. The first part, the _____, includes stories and laws that are studied and interpreted by Jewish scholars. The second part, the _____, includes the messages of the prophets and the histories of Israelite kings. The third part is called the _____ and includes stories and other writings.

Name _____ Date _____

READING SOCIAL STUDIES: GENERALIZE

(Focus Skill) Changes for the Jewish People

DIRECTIONS Complete this graphic organizer to make a generalization about how changes affected the Jewish people.

Generalize

Facts

Babylonians destroyed Jerusalem.	Judaism survived and changed.	Romans conquered Judaea.	Judaism survived under rabbi leadership.

Generalization

_____

_____

_____

_____

_____

_____

CALIFORNIA STANDARDS HSS 6.3, 6.3.4, 6.3.5

74 ■ Homework and Practice Book   Use after reading Chapter 7, pages 234–248.

Mountains and Seas

DIRECTIONS Write a paragraph that describes present-day Greece's geographical features. Use all the words from the box in your description.

isthmus	seas	mountains	peninsula	islands

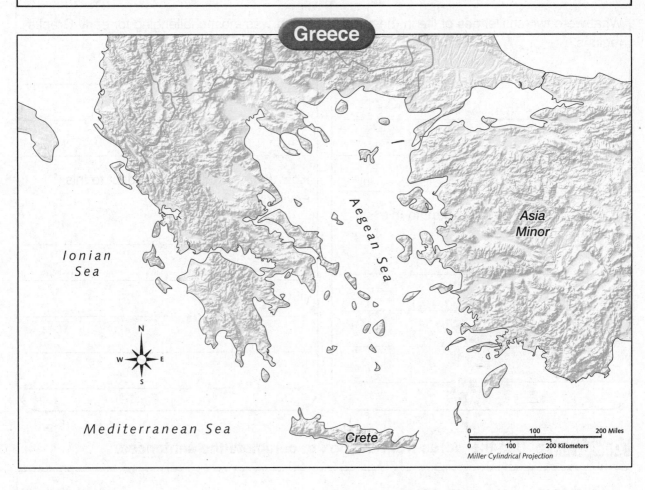

Greece

Ionian Sea

Aegean Sea

Asia Minor

Mediterranean Sea

Crete

0   100   200 Miles
0   100   200 Kilometers
Miller Cylindrical Projection

_____

_____

_____

_____

_____

_____

CALIFORNIA STANDARDS HSS 6.4, 6.4.1; CS 2, 3; HI 1, 2

(continued)

Name _____ Date _____

DIRECTIONS Answer the questions about how early Greeks adapted to their physical environments.

Life in the Mountain Regions of Greece

What were two challenges of life in these regions?

_____

_____

_____

How did the early Greeks adapt to this environment?

_____

_____

_____

Life along the Coastal Regions of Greece

What was most challenging for early Greeks in these regions?

_____

_____

How did the early Greeks adapt to this environment?

_____

_____

_____

_____

DIRECTIONS Use the words from the box to complete the sentences.

exchange	surpluses	specialize	culture	population

Early Greeks adapted to their environment to become successful farmers. This led

to an increase in _____ . Their success also resulted in food _____ . Since

not everyone needed to farm, people began to _____ in other areas. Craftworkers

could _____ their goods with farmers for food. Sharing ideas through trade also

helped develop the _____ of the early Greeks.

Use after reading Chapter 8, Lesson 1, pages 270–275.

Name _____ Date _____

Skills: Read a Population Map

DIRECTIONS Study the population density map of present-day Greece and Turkey. Then use the map to complete the activities on the following page.

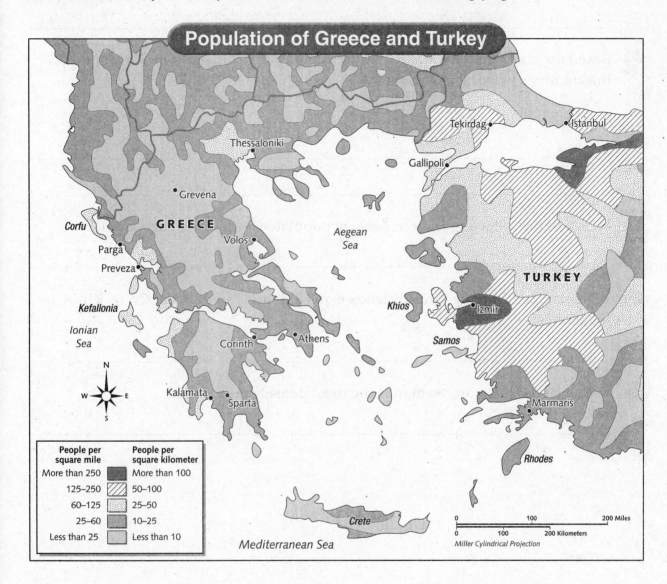

Population of Greece and Turkey

People per square mile	People per square kilometer
More than 250	More than 100
125–250	50–100
60–125	25–50
25–60	10–25
Less than 25	Less than 10

Miller Cylindrical Projection

0   100   200 Miles
0   100   200 Kilometers

CALIFORNIA STANDARDS HSS 6.4, 6.4.1; CS 3

(continued)

Name _____ Date _____

1 Write a statement that compares the population density of present-day Greece with that of Turkey as it is shown on the map.

_____

_____

2 Based on what you have learned of the geography of Greece, how do you think the country's physical environment affects its population density?

_____

_____

_____

3 Which of the following is more densely populated: Athens or Thessaloniki?

_____

4 Which of the following Greek islands is most densely populated: Crete, Khios, or Kefallonia?

_____

5 Which city or town on the map is the most densely populated?

_____

Early Civilization in Greece

DIRECTIONS Complete the chart to tell about the Minoan and Mycenaean civilizations in early Greece. Then answer the questions that follow.

	The Minoans	The Mycenaeans
Location	_____	_____
Accomplishments	• _____ _____ • _____ _____	• _____ _____ • _____ _____
Theories about how the civilization ended	_____ _____ _____ _____	_____ _____ _____ _____

1 The achievements of the early Greeks were recorded by the Greek poet Homer during the 700s B.C. How do Homer's epics contribute to our understanding of the early Greeks?

_____

_____

2 How was Greek mythology connected to the everyday lives of the early Greeks?

_____

_____

CALIFORNIA STANDARDS HSS 6.4, 6.4.1, 6.4.4

Name _____ Date _____

Skills: Compare Primary and Secondary Sources

DIRECTIONS Read the journal entry of a boy's visit to the Parthenon in Athens, Greece, and part of an encyclopedia entry on the Parthenon. Then complete the activities on the following page.

I'm really enjoying our vacation in Athens. Today we visited the Parthenon, which is on a hill called the Acropolis. It's an amazing place! The Parthenon was built during the mid-400s B.C., and it is a temple dedicated to Athena, the ancient Greek goddess of war and wisdom. You can look down from the hill and see the city of Athens.

The Parthenon is made of white marble, and the huge columns form a rectangle. Of course, the temple has suffered a lot of damage over the centuries, but it is still really something to see. As I walked around it, I tried to imagine that I was one of the ancient Greeks. I thought about how awesome it must have looked.

While I was visiting the Parthenon, I felt a real connection. It's a part of human history, and my visit there helped me understand that I'm a part of human history, too.

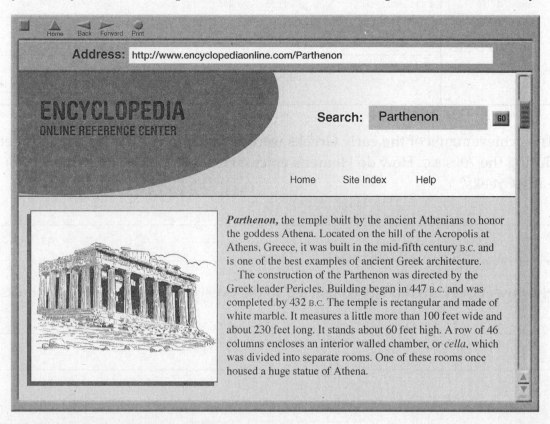

Home   Back   Forward   Print

Address: http://www.encyclopediaonline.com/Parthenon

ENCYCLOPEDIA
ONLINE REFERENCE CENTER

Search: Parthenon   GO

Home   Site Index   Help

Parthenon, the temple built by the ancient Athenians to honor the goddess Athena. Located on the hill of the Acropolis at Athens, Greece, it was built in the mid-fifth century B.C. and is one of the best examples of ancient Greek architecture.

The construction of the Parthenon was directed by the Greek leader Pericles. Building began in 447 B.C. and was completed by 432 B.C. The temple is rectangular and made of white marble. It measures a little more than 100 feet wide and about 230 feet long. It stands about 60 feet high. A row of 46 columns encloses an interior walled chamber, or *cella,* which was divided into separate rooms. One of these rooms once housed a huge statue of Athena.

 CALIFORNIA STANDARDS HSS 6.4, 6.4.4; HR 4   *(continued)*

Name _____ Date _____

1 Is the Parthenon or the excerpt from the encyclopedia article about the Parthenon a primary source? How do you know?

_____

_____

2 Why is the other source a secondary source?

_____

_____

3 Is the boy's journal entry a primary or secondary source? How do you know?

_____

_____

4 What can you learn from visiting the Parthenon that you do not learn from the encyclopedia article?

_____

_____

_____

Greek City-States

DIRECTIONS Fill in the missing information in the table about how Greek city-states developed. Then answer the questions that follow.

Development of Greek City-States
• In early Greece, each city-state was known as a polis. Each polis had an acropolis, which was a _____, and an agora, an open-air market.
• At first, each city-state was ruled as an oligarchy, in which _____ _____. This resulted in a struggle for power.
• Next, many city-states were ruled by tyrants, who ruled alone. While some had the support of their people, others became cruel and were overthrown.
• In some city-states, such as Athens, the government changed to an early form of democracy, in which _____.

1. Many Greek city-states were rivals. How did the land's geography contribute to this rivalry? What were some of the reasons Greek city-states fought against each other?

   _____

   _____

   _____

2. While city-states often fought against each other, they also had strong connections. What were these connections? How did they help all Greeks feel connected?

   _____

   _____

   _____

CALIFORNIA STANDARDS HSS 6.4, 6.4.1, 6.4.2; HI 3

Sparta and Athens

DIRECTIONS Complete each statement to show the differences between the Greek city-states of Sparta and Athens.

1 Athens was located near a harbor of the Aegean Sea, while Sparta

_____

2 In Sparta, trade and travel were discouraged, while in Athens,

_____

3 In Athens, boys attended school in order to become well-rounded citizens. In Sparta, boys

_____

DIRECTIONS Read each statement and decide whether it describes the city-state of Sparta or Athens. Write *Sparta* or *Athens* next to the statement.

4 _____ The government was ruled by an oligarchy of elders whose laws were approved by an assembly of citizens. During wartime, two kings shared authority.

5 _____ The leader Solon reformed this society by freeing farmers who had become slaves and by instituting fairer laws.

6 _____ To protect itself against its powerful neighbor and to defend against a threat from the Persian Empire, this city-state joined others in the Peloponnesian League.

7 _____ Women were highly respected and made their own decisions about their homes and families.

8 _____ A new form of democratic government allowed decisions to be made by majority rule and allowed many citizens to serve in government.

CALIFORNIA STANDARDS HSS 6.4, 6.4.1, 6.4.2, 6.4.6

Name _____ Date _____

Study Guide

DIRECTIONS Fill in the missing information in this summary. Use the terms below to help you complete the summary.

Lesson 1	Lesson 2	Lesson 3	Lesson 4
seafaring	legends	tyranny	Cyrus II
adapted	Mycenaeans	democracy	Solon
isthmus	Minoans	warfare	harbor
peninsula	mythology	oligarchy	assembly
separated	epics	commerce	inland

Lesson 1   Present-day Greece is located on a _____, which

extends out into the Mediterranean, Aegean, and Ionian Seas. A narrow

_____ connects the southern part of Greece to the mainland.

    The people who settled in the mountain valleys were _____

from each other. They _____ to the environment and became herders

and farmers. People who settled along the coasts developed _____

cultures that connected with other people in the Mediterranean.

Lesson 2   One of the earliest civilizations in Greece, the _____,

formed on the island of Crete. The _____ settled on the

Peloponnesus. The history of both civilizations lives on in stories and

_____. The Greek poet Homer composed _____ that

told of heroes and battles from early Greek history. His works also tell of the

_____ of the early Greeks who believed that gods and goddesses

controlled natural events and many aspects of human life.

CALIFORNIA STANDARDS HSS 6.4.1, 6.4.2, 6.4.4, 6.4.5, 6.4.6   *(continued)*

Name _____ Date _____

Lesson 3   The first independent city-states in Greece were often ruled by an

_____, in which a few aristocrats controlled all aspects of society and

created laws. Some of these city-states came to be ruled by a single aristocrat

who claimed power, in a form of government known as a _____.

In some city-states, these leaders were overthrown and early forms of

_____ developed, in which the government was run by citizens.

A shared Greek culture developed through _____ and through

the formation of new Greek colonies. Although the Greek city-states shared a

spoken and written language and religious beliefs, they remained rivals and

developed new forms of _____ to defend their lands and resources.

Lesson 4   The city-states of Athens and Sparta shared a heritage, but were

strikingly different from each other. Sparta's _____ location kept

it separated from other city-states. It developed a strong military. In times of

peace, an _____ of male citizens made decisions and approved laws.

Athens grew in wealth because of its location near a strong

_____. Government reforms put in place by Athenian leader

_____ marked the beginnings of democracy.

Athens and Sparta came to face a threat from the Persian Empire. Led

by _____, the Persian Empire conquered the Babylonian Empire

and much of Asia Minor, including some Greek colonies. Later, Sparta led the

Peloponnesian League of Greek city-states to defend their lands.

Name _____ Date _____

READING SOCIAL STUDIES: CAUSE AND EFFECT

(Focus Skill) **Greece's Geography**

DIRECTIONS Complete this graphic organizer to show that you understand how the geography of Greece affected Greek civilization.

Cause and Effect

Cause	Effect
Cause Mountains cover most of mainland Greece.	**Effect** _____ _____
Cause Greece has many fine harbors.	**Effect** _____ _____
Cause Greece's soil is mostly rocky, and its climate is dry.	**Effect** _____ _____

CALIFORNIA STANDARDS HSS 6.4, 6.4.1; HI 2

Use after reading Chapter 8, pages 270–303.

A Time of Glory in Athens

DIRECTIONS Complete the activities that follow about the Persian War.

1 Why did Greek city-states form the Delian League?

_____

_____

2 Describe one battle in the Persian War in which the Athenians played a key role.

_____

_____

_____

3 Describe the role Sparta played in the Persian War.

_____

_____

DIRECTIONS Use the organizer to show the differences between a direct democracy and a representative democracy.

Direct Democracy	Representative Democracy
How it works: _____ _____ _____ Best suited for: _____ _____ Example of a government run as a direct democracy: _____ _____	How it works: _____ _____ _____ Best suited for: _____ _____ Example of a government run as a representative democracy: _____ _____

 CALIFORNIA STANDARDS HSS 6.4, 6.4.2, 6.4.3, 6.4.5, 6.4.6

Name _____ Date _____

Skills: Read a Circle Graph

DIRECTIONS Study the circle graph about employment in Greece in 2002. Then use the graph to answer the questions.

Employment in Greece in 2002

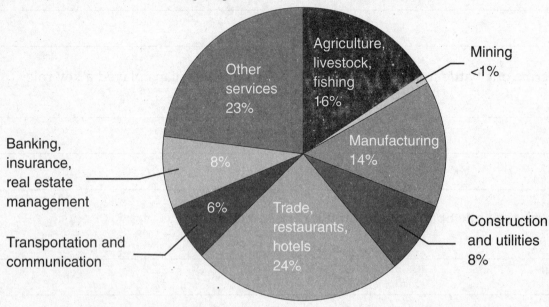

1. Which field had the greatest number of employees in Greece in 2002?

   _____

2. Which field had the fewest number of employees in Greece in 2002?

   _____

3. In 2002, were more people employed in manufacturing or in agriculture, livestock, and fishing?

   _____

4. Which two fields together employed about half of Greece's work force in 2002?

   _____

5. Which two fields employed the same percentage of people in 2002?

   _____

   _____

CALIFORNIA STANDARDS HSS 6.4; CS 3

© Harcourt

Greek Gifts

DIRECTIONS The art and architecture of ancient Greece have had a lasting influence on the world. In the space below, explain what Greek art and architecture tell about the ancient Greeks' values, religious beliefs, and their daily lives.

1 _____
_____
_____
_____
_____
_____

DIRECTIONS Write the name of an important figure from Greek literature and theater from the box to match each statement.

Aristophanes	Hesiod	Sophocles	Aesop

2 _____ The tragedies written by this playwright are still performed today.

3 _____ This poet's epic poems described Greek mythology and life in ancient Greece.

4 _____ His fables, such as "The Hare and the Tortoise," are still used today to teach morals.

5 _____ This playwright's comedies used humor to tell about serious ideas.

CALIFORNIA STANDARDS HSS 6.4, 6.4.4, 6.4.8; HR1, 2 *(continued)*

Name _____ Date _____

DIRECTIONS Choose two of the figures from ancient Greece listed in the box below. In the spaces provided, tell about each man's contributions to the fields of science, mathematics, education, law, or philosophy. Then complete the activities that follow.

Pythagoras	Plato	Democritus	Aristotle	Hippocrates

6 _____

_____

_____

7 _____

_____

8 The Greek historian Thucydides wrote about the rivalry between Athens and Sparta from a unique perspective. How did his writing contribute to the way that history is written?

_____

_____

9 In what ways did some Greek thinkers challenge the ideas of their time?

_____

_____

_____

10 Imagine that you are a Greek citizen of Athens and that Socrates has just been sentenced to death. What is your opinion of this sentence?

_____

_____

_____

Use after reading Chapter 9, Lesson 2, pages 324–331.

Name _____ Date _____

Times of Conflict

DIRECTIONS Answer the following questions about conflicts between Athens and Sparta. Use the boxed words in your answer to each question.

1 Why did Sparta feel threatened by Athens during the 400s B.C.? What happened as a result?

Delian League	Thirty Years' Peace

_____

_____

_____

2 After Athens surrendered to Sparta in 404 B.C., what changes did Sparta bring to the government of Athens?

dictatorship	the Thirty Tyrants

_____

_____

_____

3 How did Athens regain its independence?

Thebes	refused	the Three Thousand

_____

_____

_____

4 What role did Thebes play in this period of unrest among the city-states?

Peloponnesian League	democracy

_____

_____

_____

_____

CALIFORNIA STANDARDS HSS 6.4, 6.4.2, 6.4.6; HI 1

Name _____ Date _____

Skills: Resolve Conflicts

DIRECTIONS Read about a fictional conflict between a father and his son in ancient Greece. Then complete the activities that follow.

My son wants to go to Athens to attend the Lyceum school and to study under the great thinker Aristotle. I do not want him to go. He would be gone for two years! I am a successful farmer, and he is my only son. While I admire Aristotle, I believe the school is better suited for those who can afford to leave their responsibilities behind. I have no one I can depend on to help me, and our family will suffer.

I want my father to see that my desire to attend the Lyceum is not a whim. I feel a great need to learn more about our world, and in these times of great changes and unrest, I believe I could make a great contribution. But I must expand my knowledge, and where better to do so than the Lyceum? When I return, I will bring with me new ideas and skills that will improve our lives!

What seems to be the main reason the father does not want his son to attend the Lyceum?

_____

Why does the son think that attending the Lyceum will help his family?

_____

_____

Describe two possible compromises that could help resolve this conflict.

• _____

_____

• _____

_____

Which compromise do you think is better? Explain your answer.

_____

_____

CALIFORNIA STANDARDS HSS 6.4, 6.4.8; HR 5

92 ▪ **Homework and Practice Book**   Use after reading Chapter 9, Skill Lesson, pages 342–343.

Alexander Builds an Empire

DIRECTIONS Number the events below in the order in which they occurred.

1 ___ Alexander and his powerful army conquer lands in Asia Minor, Egypt, the Persian Empire, and India.

2 ___ Phillip II of Macedonia conquers and unites the Greek city-states.

3 ___ The Romans gain control of Mediterranean lands.

4 ___ After battles are fought over control, the great empire splits into the kingdoms of Macedonia, Syria, and Egypt.

DIRECTIONS Write the name of the Hellenistic scholar from the box to complete each statement. Then answer the question that follows.

Eratosthenes	Archimedes	Hypatia	Aristarchus	Euclid

5 The astronomer _____ used mathematical ideas to estimate the diameter and circumference of Earth.

6 The inventor _____ used mathematics to invent machines.

7 The astronomer _____ studied Earth's rotation and orbit around the sun.

8 The mathematician _____ is known as the father of geometry.

9 The mathematician _____ was also a philosopher who started a school of philosophy in Alexandria.

10 Why did Alexander the Great have a deep appreciation for Greek culture? How did he bring Greek culture to the lands he conquered?

_____

_____

_____

_____

CALIFORNIA STANDARDS HSS 6.4, 6.4.7, 6.4.8; HI 1

Skills: Read a Time Zone Map

DIRECTIONS Study the time zone map on this page. Then complete the activities on the following page.

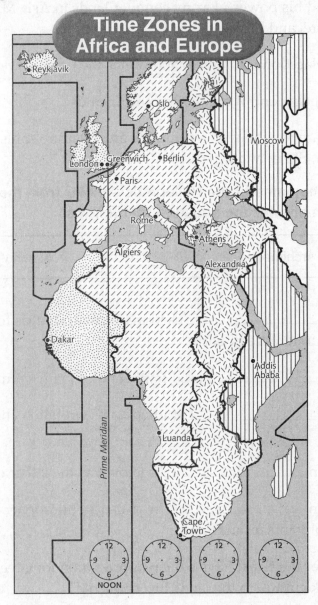

Time Zones in Africa and Europe

CALIFORNIA STANDARDS HSS 6.4; CS 3

(continued)

94 ■ Homework and Practice Book   Use after reading Chapter 9, Skill Lesson, pages 352–353.

Name _____ Date _____

1 Through which city does the prime meridian pass? Why is this line of longitude important?

_____

_____

_____

2 Draw hands on the clocks to show the time in each time zone when it is 12:00 noon at the prime meridian. Label the clocks A.M. or P.M.

_____

_____

3 When it is 10:00 A.M. in Athens, what time is it in Rome? _____

4 With which city on the map does Moscow share a time zone? _____

5 When it is 1:00 A.M. in Oslo, what time is it in Dakar? _____

6 When it is 1:00 P.M. in Alexandria, what time is it in Reykjavik? _____

7 When it is 12:00 midnight in London, what time is it in Athens? _____

8 With which cities on the map does Cape Town share a time zone? _____

_____

9 Imagine that the time zone map included one more zone to the west. What time

would be shown on the clock for that zone? _____

10 Explain why time zone boundaries do not always follow the meridians.

_____

_____

_____

Name _____ Date _____

Study Guide

DIRECTIONS Fill in the missing information in this article. Use the terms below to help you complete the article.

Lesson 1	Lesson 2	Lesson 3	Lesson 4
Delian League	theater	the Thirty Tyrants	Macedonia
Pericles	Socrates	the Peloponnesian War	Hellenistic Age
Golden Age	Hesiod		Persia
Darius I	Thucydides	Thebes	Archimedes
tributes	architecture	the Thirty Years' Peace	Alexandria

Lesson 1   The history of ancient Greece is one of wars, conquest, and great

cultural achievements. While Greek city-states battled each other for control, a

common threat united them during the 400s B.C. The leader of the Persian Empire,

_____ , had invaded Greek cities in Asia Minor. In the years

that followed, Athens and 150 other Greek city-states joined forces to fight off the

Persians. With its powerful navy, Athens led the _____ .

   After the Persian War, Athens grew even stronger. _____

from other city-states made Athens wealthy. Under the leader

_____ , the city became a center of the arts, learning, and

culture. This time became known as the _____ of Athens.

Lesson 2   The ancient Greeks are credited with many contributions

still appreciated today. The methods and meaning behind Greek

_____ can be seen in many modern buildings. The ideas

presented in Greek _____ still entertain and enlighten

audiences today. The work of the poet _____ helps modern

CALIFORNIA STANDARDS HSS 6.4, 6.4.2, 6.4.4, 6.4.5, 6.4.6, 6.4.7, 6.4.8   (continued)

96 ▪ Homework and Practice Book   Use after reading Chapter 9, pages 314–350.

Lesson 2 (*continued*)   scholars understand the lives and beliefs of the ancient Greeks. The historian _____ recorded events in a factual way that provides a model for modern writers. Great philosophers such as _____ and Aristotle developed ways of thinking that influenced the ideas of later Western civilizations.

Lesson 3   Conflicts between Athens and Sparta grew more intense, and war between the two city-states broke out in 460 B.C. After 15 years of fighting, Athens and Sparta signed an agreement known as _____.

Not long afterward, battles broke out again and Athens and Sparta fought each other for the next 27 years. Eventually, Sparta controlled Athens and replaced Athens's democracy with a dictatorship ruled by _____. The cruelty of this rule caused _____ and other city-states to work together to restore democracy to Athens. By the end of _____, city-states were weakened and unstable.

Lesson 4   Phillip II, the king of _____, conquered and united the Greek city-states. His son Alexander hoped to fulfill his father's dream of conquering _____ and the rest of the world as he knew it. By 331 B.C., Alexander controlled a vast empire that extended eastward to India.

Alexander brought Greek culture to all areas of his empire and modeled new cities after Greek city-states. The most famous city was _____, located in Egypt. As culture and learning blossomed, great figures emerged from the _____. Thinkers such as Hypatia, Euclid, and _____ spread new ideas throughout Alexander's empire.

READING SOCIAL STUDIES: CAUSE AND EFFECT

Focus Skill **The Golden Age**

DIRECTIONS Complete this graphic organizer to show that you understand why Athens became the model for respected political, economic and social structures for all of Greece.

Cause and Effect

Cause

_____

_____

_____

Effect

Athens experiences many cultural achievements.

Cause

Pericles wants to make Athens a center for art and learning.

Effect

_____

_____

_____

Cause

Greeks, such as Socrates, Plato, and Aristotle, begin questioning old ways of thinking.

Effect

_____

_____

_____

 CALIFORNIA STANDARDS HSS 6.4, 6.4.8; HI 2

Indus Valley Civilization

DIRECTIONS Complete each category in the organizer to describe the early Indus River valley civilization.

Geographic Location	Indus River Valley Civilization	Seasonal Factors

Agriculture	Planned Cities	Trade

CALIFORNIA STANDARDS HSS 6.5, 6.5.1; HI 1

Name _____ Date _____

Skills: Follow a Flowchart

DIRECTIONS Milk has been an important part of the diet on the Indian subcontinent for centuries. Making fresh Indian cheeses, called *chenna* and *paneer*, is a fairly simple process. Study the flowchart that tells how they are made. Then complete the activities on the following page.

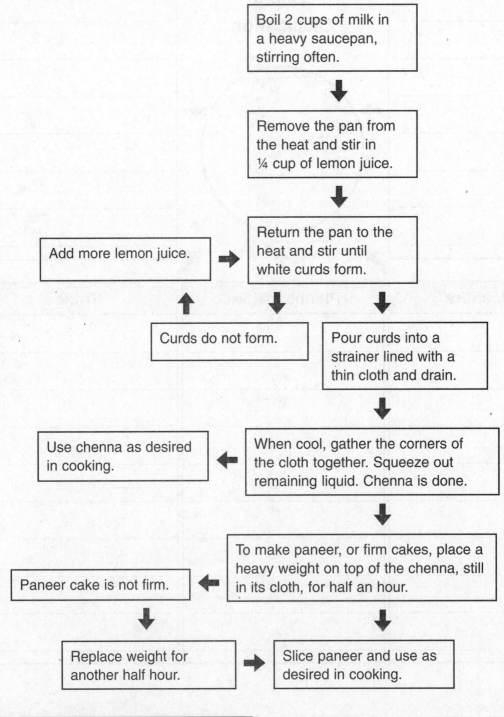

CALIFORNIA STANDARDS HSS 6.5; CS 3

(continued)

100 ■ Homework and Practice Book   Use after reading Chapter 10, Skill Lesson, pages 380–381.

Name _____ Date _____

1 What is the central idea for the flowchart?

_____

_____

_____

2 What should happen if curds do not form? What is this type of situation on a flowchart called?

_____

_____

_____

_____

3 Describe the two choices of what to do with the chenna once it is prepared.

_____

_____

_____

_____

_____

4 Which step comes first—straining the curds or placing a heavy weight on the chenna?

_____

5 What might happen if a reader did not pay attention to the direction in which arrows point on a flowchart?

_____

_____

_____

_____

_____

_____

Beginnings of Hinduism

DIRECTIONS It is believed that the Aryans began to arrive on the Indian subcontinent in about 1500 B.C. In the space provided, describe three theories about their origins in this region.

1 _____

_____

2 _____

_____

3 _____

_____

DIRECTIONS Use the words from the box to complete the statements about the Aryans and their influences on Indian culture.

dharma	Bhagavad Gita	Mahabharata	Vedas
raja	Sanskrit	Brahmanas	

4 The Aryan religion was based on the _____, some of which are the oldest known religious writings.

5 In Hinduism, religious duty is known as _____.

6 The Aryan story called the _____ is the longest epic poem ever written.

7 The tribes of early Aryans were ruled by a _____, a chief priest, and a ruling council.

8 Many modern Indian languages come from _____, which was brought to the region by the Aryans.

9 The Vedas describe important rituals for priests to follow in the

_____.

10 In the part of the *Mahabharata* known as the _____, a god speaks to a Vedic warrior about following established duties.

CALIFORNIA STANDARDS HSS 6.5, 6.5.2, 6.5.3, 6.5.4, 6.5.7; HI 2   *(continued)*

102 ▪ Homework and Practice Book   Use after reading Chapter 10, Lesson 2, pages 384–389.

Name _____ Date _____

DIRECTIONS Complete the chart to describe the Indian social classes.

India's Social Classes

Class	Related to What Part(s) of the Human Body	Members of This Class
Brahmans	_____	_____ _____
Kshatriyas	_____ _____	_____
Vaisyas	_____ _____	_____
Sudras	_____ _____	_____

DIRECTIONS Complete the web to tell about the basic ideas of Hinduism.

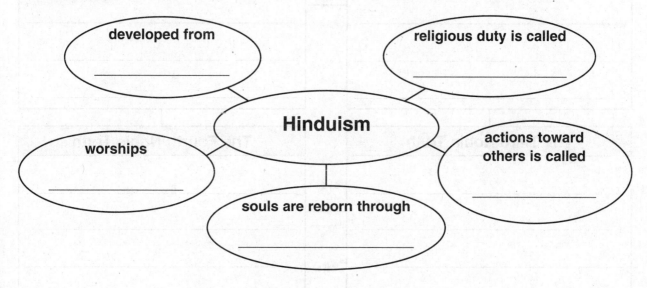

The Beginning of Buddhism

DIRECTIONS Answer the questions about the roots of Buddhism. Then complete the organizer to tell about Buddhist ideas.

1 How did Siddhartha Gautama's upbringing influence his religious ideas and cause him to search for answers?

_____

_____

_____

_____

2 How did the idea of reincarnation from Hinduism lead to Siddhartha Gautama's forming of Buddhism?

_____

_____

The Four Noble Truths

The First Noble Truth	The Second Noble Truth

The Third Noble Truth	The Fourth Noble Truth

CALIFORNIA STANDARDS HSS 6.5, 6.5.5; HI 3

(continued)

Name _____ Date _____

The Buddhist Eightfold Path is often symbolized by a wheel. Complete the wheel to describe the steps of the Eightfold Path. Then answer the questions that follow.

The Eightfold Path

right thought _____

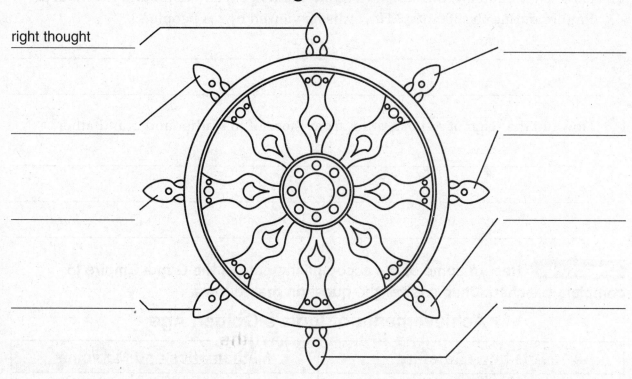

1. The religion of Jainism was formed during the 500s B.C. in India by Vardhamana Mahavira. How did his ideas about peaceful action come to influence others?

_____

_____

_____

2. What are some of the ideas that Hinduism, Buddhism, and Jainism share?

_____

_____

3. How did the ideas of Buddhism spread through India?

_____

_____

Empires of India

DIRECTIONS Answer the questions that follow about the Maurya Empire.

1 How did the Indian ruler Chandragupta Maurya expand and build the Maurya Empire during the 300s B.C.? How was he viewed by his people?

_____

_____

2 How did the reign of Ashoka differ from those of his father and grandfather?

_____

_____

_____

DIRECTIONS Record some of the accomplishments of the Gupta Empire to complete the chart. Then answer the question that follows.

Achievements of India's Golden Age

Arts and Literature	Mathematics and Medicine
• government support of arts and artists	• _____
• _____	
	• _____
• _____	
	• _____
• _____	
	• _____

Which achievement do you think was the most important? Tell why you think so.

_____

_____

CALIFORNIA STANDARDS HSS 6.5, 6.5.6, 6.5.7

Skills: Act as a Responsible Citizen

DIRECTIONS Read the passage below about Mohandas
Gandhi. Then answer the questions that follow.

Mohandas Gandhi lived from 1869 to 1948 and was seen
as one of the most influential spiritual and political leaders
of his time. His work to free India from British rule through
nonviolence inspired countless people.

Gandhi believed in leading a simple life and felt deeply
that one must develop great courage in order to be nonviolent. He developed the idea of *satyagraha*, or "the devotion to
truth." This nonviolent approach to truth included the belief
that the way people behave is more important than what they
achieve. Gandhi believed that *satyagraha* could be followed in
one person's daily life as well as on a larger political scale.

Gandhi worked tirelessly to resist laws that he felt were unfair and spent years in
prison as a result. He organized strikes and boycotts to bring reforms, and helped inform
millions of people through his efforts. While he often disagreed with British leaders, the
British government remembered his efforts by erecting a statue in his honor in 1969.

1 Why do you think Mohandas Gandhi is seen as a great leader?

_____

2 How do you think nonviolence helps a person act as a responsible citizen?

_____

_____

3 What were some of the actions that Gandhi took to bring change?

_____

_____

4 In his idea of *satyagraha*, Gandhi believed that the way people behave is more
important than what they achieve. Do you agree or disagree? Explain your answer.

_____

_____

CALIFORNIA STANDARDS HSS 6.5; HI 2

Chapter 10 Study Guide

DIRECTIONS Fill in the missing information in this summary. Use the terms below to help you complete the summary.

Lesson 1	Lesson 2	Lesson 3	Lesson 4
grid	Hinduism	Siddhartha Gautama	Kalinga
granaries	caste	Vardhamana Mahavira	Golden Age
subcontinent	Vedas	reincarnation	Chandragupta I
monsoon	Sanskrit	nonviolence	Gupta
citadel			Ashoka

Lesson 1   The Indus River valley provided fertile lands for ancient civilizations to form on the Indian _____. Early farmers faced serious challenges, including flooding during summer months caused by the seasonal _____. By about 2500 B.C., success in agriculture had led to increased populations and the formation of cities. Early cities, such as Mohenjo-Daro, Harappa, and Lothal were well planned and highly organized. Each city was laid out in a _____ and included a _____ that housed buildings used for governmental and religious purposes and _____ for storing food. Although trade between these cities and with places as far away as Mesopotamia flourished, the Harappan civilization declined after 1750 B.C.

Lesson 2   In about 1500 B.C., people known as Aryans migrated to the region. While there are several theories about their migration, their language, _____, is the root of many modern Indian languages. Their religious beliefs are found in the _____ that had been passed

 CALIFORNIA STANDARDS HSS 6.5, 6.5.1, 6.5.2, 6.5.3, 6.5.4, 6.5.5, 6.5.6, 6.5.7   *(continued)*

108 ■ Homework and Practice Book   Use after reading Chapter 10, pages 374–402.

Lesson 2 *(continued)*   down orally for hundreds of years. The religion of

_____ later developed from this Aryan religion. The Aryans

developed a social _____ system, which determined how

people could live.

Lesson 3   In the 500s B.C., a young Indian prince named

_____ introduced new religious ideas. After years

of seeking answers, he believed that human suffering and the cycle of

_____ could be broken if people were good and

pure and followed moral ways. He became known as the Buddha, and

his ideas founded the religion of Buddhism. Another religion, known as

Jainism, was founded by _____ during the

500s B.C. and shared many ideas with Buddhism. Jainism emphasizes

using _____ to bring about change.

Lesson 4   In about 320 B.C., the Indian city-states were united by

Chandragupta Maurya. Under his rule, the Maurya Empire grew, but he

and his son were harsh and cruel. His grandson, _____,

also expanded the empire, but after he conquered the kingdom of

_____ he rejected violence and became a Buddhist.

   A new empire formed in about A.D. 320, led by _____.

The _____ Empire brought a time of peace and great cultural

achievements, which became known as India's _____.

READING SOCIAL STUDIES: COMPARE AND CONTRAST

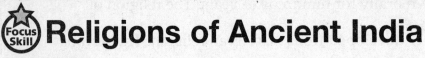

Religions of Ancient India

DIRECTIONS Complete this graphic organizer to compare and contrast information about ancient India.

Compare and Contrast

Topic 1

Hinduism:
belief in many gods, caste system

Similar
_____
_____

Topic 2

Buddhism:
focus not on gods, no caste system

Topic 1

Buddhism:
Eightfold Path

Similar
_____
_____

Topic 2

Jainism:
path of the "three jewels"

CALIFORNIA STANDARDS HSS 6.5, 6.5.3, 6.5.4, 6.5.5, 6.5.7

110 ■ Homework and Practice Book   Use after reading Chapter 10, pages 374–402.

The Landscape of China

DIRECTIONS Use each pair of terms to write a sentence that describes China's geographic features.

1 western China   steppes

_____

_____

2 Huang He   loess

_____

_____

3 central China   Gobi

_____

_____

4 geographic barriers   isolated

_____

_____

DIRECTIONS Use the names from the box to complete the sentences about ancient Chinese legends.

| Yu the Great | Xilingshi | Huang Di | Shen Nong |

5 One Chinese legend tells how _____ invented silk cloth.

6 The legend of _____ describes how he dug deep canals to save China from terrible floods.

7 The legends about _____ say that he studied agriculture and became the father of traditional Chinese medicine.

8 According to many Chinese legends, _____ ordered the invention of Chinese writing.

CALIFORNIA STANDARDS HSS 6.6, 6.6.1, 6.6.2

Name _____ Date _____

Skills: Read a Climograph

DIRECTIONS Study the climograph for Hong Kong. Then answer the following questions.

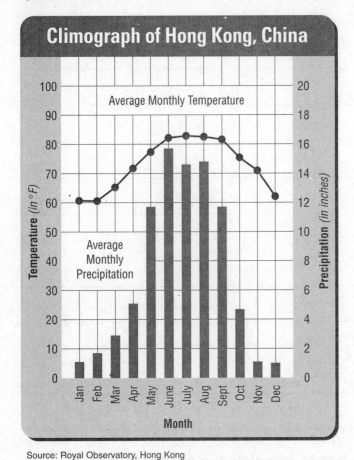

Climograph of Hong Kong, China

Source: Royal Observatory, Hong Kong

1 Which is the warmest month?

_____

2 Which is the wettest month?

_____

3 Which month receives the least precipitation?

_____

4 What is the average monthly temperature in May?

_____

5 Which two months have the lowest temperatures?

_____

6 What is the average monthly precipitation in December?

7 Which three-month period has both the highest temperatures and the highest precipitation?

_____

CALIFORNIA STANDARDS HSS 6.6; CS 3

112 ■ **Homework and Practice Book**   Use after reading Chapter 11, Skill Lesson, pages 420–421.

Early Chinese Civilization

DIRECTIONS Complete the web to tell about the Shang dynasty and the origins of Chinese civilization. Then answer the questions that follow.

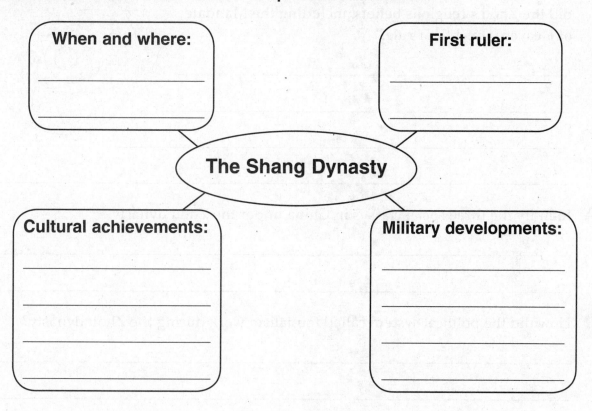

When and where:

_____

_____

First ruler:

_____

The Shang Dynasty

Cultural achievements:

_____

_____

_____

_____

Military developments:

_____

_____

_____

_____

Why did Shang kings use oracle bones? What does the writing on oracle bones tell us about the Shang dynasty?

_____

_____

_____

_____

CALIFORNIA STANDARDS HSS 6.6, 6.6.1, 6.6.3, 5.6.4; CS 3   *(continued)*

Name _____ Date _____

Complete the activities to tell about the times of
the Zhou dynasty.

1 In about 1122 B.C., the Zhou conquered the Shang. How
did the Zhou's religious beliefs, including the Mandate
of Heaven, affect their rule?

_____

_____

_____

_____

2 Identify the three social classes in China under the Zhou dynasty.

_____

_____

3 How did the political system called feudalism work during the Zhou dynasty?

_____

_____

_____

4 What were Confucius's main teachings about how people should behave?

_____

_____

_____

5 How are the ideas of Daoism like those of Confucianism? How are they different?

_____

_____

_____

_____

Uniting China

DIRECTIONS Complete the organizer to tell about the Qin dynasty under Shi Huangdi. Then answer the questions that follow.

The Qin Dynasty Under Shi Huangdi
221 B.C.–206 B.C.

What was the governing system known as Legalism like under Shi Huangdi?	How did a strong bureaucracy support Shi Huangdi's government?	What systems of standardization did Shi Huangdi set up?

1 How did Shi Huangdi's wall support the Qin empire?

_____

_____

_____

2 In what way does Shi Huangdi's tomb tell about the importance of the military during his rule?

_____

_____

CALIFORNIA STANDARDS HSS 6.6, 6.6.5; HI 2

Skills: Identify Changing Borders

DIRECTIONS Study the maps below. One shows the borders of China during the Qin dynasty. The other shows the borders of present-day China. Then complete the following activities.

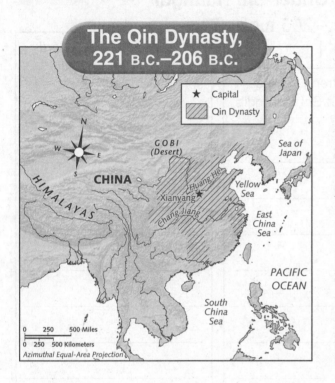

1 Which natural landform marks the northern border of China during the Qin dynasty and present-day China?

_____

_____

2 Which natural landform is a part of China today but was not a part of China during the Qin dynasty?

_____

_____

CALIFORNIA STANDARDS HSS 6.6, 6.6.2; CS 3   (*continued*)

116 ■ Homework and Practice Book   Use after reading Chapter 11, Skill Lesson, pages 440–441.

3 What major rivers run through both China during the Qin dynasty and present-day China?

_____

_____

4 Describe the location of the Qin dynasty's capital city and the capital city of present-day China.

_____

_____

_____

_____

5 How does the southeast border of present-day China compare with that of China during the Qin dynasty?

_____

_____

_____

_____

6 Write a statement that compares the borders of present-day China with the borders of China during the Qin dynasty.

_____

_____

_____

_____

A Time of Achievement

DIRECTIONS The Han dynasty ruled China for more than 400 years. Complete the sentences to describe the strengths of the Han dynasty.

1 Emperors during the Han dynasty combined Legalist and Confucian ideas to rule

the empire. This was important because these ideas _____

_____

2 The Han emperor Wu Di created huge armies during his rule. This was important

because _____

DIRECTIONS Complete the organizer about the importance of the Silk Road. Use the words from the box to help you complete the organizer.

Buddhism	Europe

The Silk Road

- _____
  _____

- _____
  _____
  _____

- _____
  _____

- _____
  _____

CALIFORNIA STANDARDS HSS 6.6, 6.6.6, 6.6.7, 6.6.8; HI 3

118 ■ Homework and Practice Book   Use after reading Chapter 11, Lesson 4, pages 442–446.

Name _____ Date _____

Study Guide

DIRECTIONS Fill in the missing information in this summary. Use the terms below to help you complete the summary.

Lesson 1	Lesson 2	Lesson 3	Lesson 4
Yu the Great	virtue	standardization	Wu Di
terraces	Confucius	protection	Silk Road
barriers	Tang the Successful	bureaucracy	Gaozu
Shen Nong	feudalism	Legalism	civil service

Lesson 1   The people of ancient China settled along two great rivers, the

Huang He and the Chang Jiang. The Huang He is known for the yellow

silt, or loess, that colors the water. In the Chang Jiang Valley, farmers built

_____ to hold in water. Mountains and deserts formed natural

_____ that isolated the land from the rest of the world.

Chinese legends tell of the heroic deeds of ancient rulers, such as

_____, who is said to have dug great canals to save China

from floods. Another legend tells of the ruler _____, who is

said to have introduced agriculture to ancient China.

Lesson 2   The Shang dynasty began under the rule of _____

who united the villages of the Huang He Valley. This dynasty brought

many advances to the area, including the first writing system and new

military technologies. The Shang were conquered by the Zhou, who

believed that they would have control of China as long as they showed

_____. The Zhou dynasty developed the political system

CALIFORNIA STANDARDS HSS 6.6, 6.6.1, 6.6.2, 6.6.3, 6.6.4, 6.6.5, 6.6.6, 6.6.7   *(continued)*

Lesson 2 *(continued)*   of _____ , in which land was exchanged

for loyalty. The philosopher _____ spent his life spreading

his ideas about honor and respect.

Lesson 3   In 221 B.C., Shi Huangdi became China's first emperor by uniting

China under the Qin Empire. He ruled under a governing system called

_____ , which gave him absolute power. To control his

empire efficiently, Shi Huangdi created a _____ to manage

his provinces. He also began a policy of _____ , in which

money, writing, and education helped unify the empire. Shi Huangdi

also unified the empire by connecting existing walls along its borders for

_____ from enemies.

Lesson 4   In 202 B.C., the Han dynasty came to control China, led by the

emperor _____ . The Han ruled for more than 400 years by

combining Legalist and Confucian ideas. The emperor _____

greatly expanded the empire with his strong military forces. He also set up

China's first _____ , in which educated people could be

picked for government jobs.

   The many cultural achievements of the Han dynasty led to China's

Golden Age. New ideas and goods were also exchanged by way of the

_____ , which connected China and Europe.

Name _____ Date _____

READING SOCIAL STUDIES: COMPARE AND CONTRAST

(Focus Skill) **Dynasties of Ancient China**

DIRECTIONS Complete this graphic organizer to compare and contrast the dynasties of ancient China.

Compare and Contrast

Topic 1

Qin dynasty: lasted only 15 years; followed Legalism

Similar

_____

_____

_____

Topic 2

Han dynasty: lasted more than 400 years; followed Confucianism and Legalism

Topic 1

Zhou dynasty: introduced money in the form of coins and written laws to China

Similar

_____

_____

Topic 2

Shang dynasty: invented a writing system using characters

CALIFORNIA STANDARDS HSS 6.6, 6.6.3, 6.6.4, 6.6.5, 6.6.6

The Founding of Rome

DIRECTIONS Complete the organizer to identify the people who settled on the Italian Peninsula, and explain how they used the region's geographic features.

Farming: _____
_____
_____

Defense: _____
_____
_____

Settling the Italian Peninsula

Trade: _____
_____
_____

Culture groups: _____
_____
_____

DIRECTIONS Use the names and terms from the box to complete the following statements about early Roman history.

assembly	Remus	Tarquinius Priscus
Romulus	Forum	confederation

1 The Etruscans created a _____ of 12 city-states that worked together and had similar governments.

2 The city of Rome was named after its first ruler, _____.

3 During the mid-600s B.C., Roman kings were elected to rule by an

_____ made up of Rome's leading male citizens.

4 The flat land of the _____ was used by the Romans as a place to exchange goods and ideas.

5 According to legend, _____ argued with his twin brother about where to build a new settlement on the Tiber River.

6 The first Etruscan king of Rome, _____, began many building projects during his rule.

CALIFORNIA STANDARDS HSS 6.7, 6.7.1

Use after reading Chapter 12, Lesson 1, pages 468–473.

Skills: Compare Maps with Different Scales

DIRECTIONS Study the map of central Rome and the map of Italy. Then use the maps to complete the activities that follow.

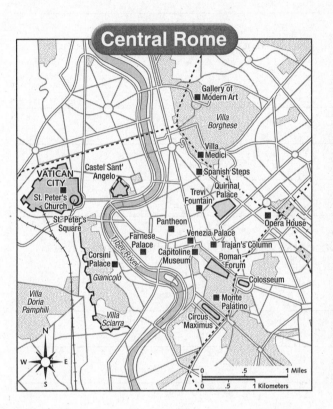

1 How are the maps different? How are they alike?

_____

_____

_____

_____

Name _____ Date _____

2 Which map's scale gives you a clearer idea of the size of the city of Rome? Why?

_____

_____

_____

3 Which map would you use to determine the distance between Rome and Genoa? Why?

_____

_____

_____

4 Locate the Tiber River on both maps. Describe what each map shows about the Tiber River.

_____

_____

_____

5 Which map would you use to determine the distance between the Roman Forum and St. Peter's Church in Vatican City? Why?

_____

_____

_____

The Roman Republic

DIRECTIONS Complete the organizer to tell about the government of the Roman Republic. Then answer the questions that follow.

The Roman Tripartite Government

_____

Who they were: two men, elected each year

What they did: _____

_____

_____

Who served in it: 300 leading Roman men

What they did: _____

_____

_____

Who served in them: all adult male citizens

What they did: _____

_____

1 What is a republic? _____

_____

2 Why was the Roman government divided into three parts? _____

_____

3 How did the Roman government change during emergencies? _____

_____

_____

CALIFORNIA STANDARDS HSS 6.7, 6.7.2; HI 1

(continued)

Name _____ Date _____

DIRECTIONS Ancient Roman society had two main social classes, the patricians and the plebeians. Tell who made up each class, and describe their roles in society.

4 The patrician class: _____

_____

_____

5 The plebeian class: _____

_____

_____

_____

DIRECTIONS Imagine that you are a member of the plebeian class in 450 B.C. Tell about your point of view in the answer to the questions that follow.

6 Why did the plebeians make a decision in 494 B.C. to refuse to fight for Rome?

_____

_____

_____

_____

7 How do you feel about gaining the right to elect tribunes?

_____

_____

8 How do you feel about the display of the Twelve Tables?

_____

_____

Roman Expansion

DIRECTIONS Complete the time line, using the choices listed below. Next to each marker on the time line, write the letter of the correct event.

Roman Control Expands

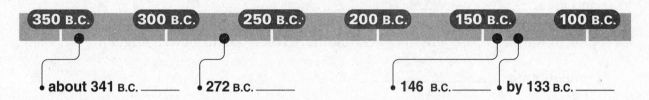

350 B.C.   300 B.C.   250 B.C.   200 B.C.   150 B.C.   100 B.C.

• about 341 B.C. _____   • 272 B.C. _____   • 146 B.C. _____ • by 133 B.C. _____

A. As victor of the Punic Wars against Carthage, Rome extends its power to provinces in Africa.

B. Rome rules the Italian Peninsula.

C. Rome controls nearly all of the lands surrounding the Mediterranean Sea.

D. Rome began to expand its territory on the Italian Peninsula.

DIRECTIONS Use the terms from the box to complete the following sentences.

Pausanias	Pergamum	Hannibal	Roman Lake	Scipio

1 King Attalus III spared _____ from war by peacefully turning over his country to the Romans.

2 In the Second Punic War, a surprise attack on Rome was led by

_____ , who came through Spain and over the Alps.

3 The Greek historian _____ told of how Mummius led the Romans to defeat and plunder Corinth.

4 In the Battle of Zama, _____ led the Romans to victory over the Carthaginians.

5 The Mediterranean Sea became known as the _____ when Rome controlled nearly all of the lands around it.

CALIFORNIA STANDARDS HSS 6.7, 6.7.3; CS 2

Skills: Read a Cartogram

DIRECTIONS Study the political map and the population cartogram of Europe on the following page. Then use them to complete the activities below.

1 Look at Italy and Portugal on the political map. Which country has a larger

land area? _____

2 Look at Italy and Sweden on the cartogram. Which country has a larger

population? _____

3 Look at Belgium and Bulgaria on the political map. Which country has a larger

area? _____

4 Look at Belgium and Bulgaria on the cartogram. Which country has a larger

population? _____

5 Write a sentence that compares the population and land areas of Belgium and

Bulgaria. _____

_____

6 France is Europe's largest country. Write a sentence that compares France's
population and land areas with those of another European country.

_____

_____

7 Describe how studying the cartogram of Europe and the political map of Europe
together gives you more information about the continent.

_____

_____

_____

CALIFORNIA STANDARDS HSS 6.7; CS 3   *(continued)*

128 ■ **Homework and Practice Book**   Use after reading Chapter 12, Skill Lesson, pages 490–491.

Political Map of Europe

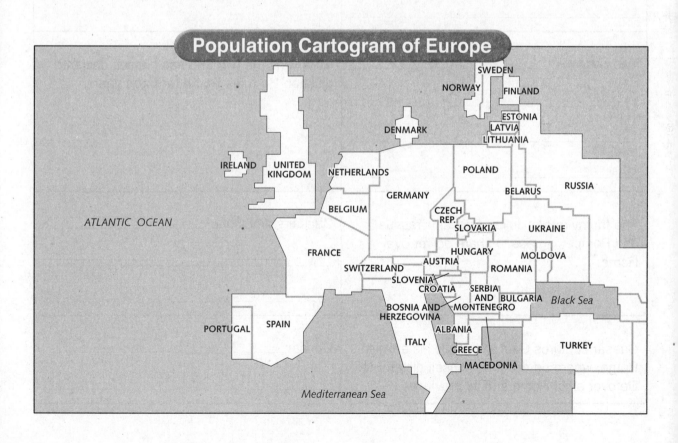

FINLAND

NORWAY SWEDEN

ESTONIA

RUSSIA

LATVIA

ATLANTIC OCEAN

DENMARK

LITHUANIA

IRELAND

NETHERLANDS

RUSSIA BELARUS

UNITED
KINGDOM

POLAND

GERMANY

BELGIUM

LUX.

UKRAINE

0   250   500 Miles

0   250   500 Kilometers

Albers Equal-Area Projection

CZECH REP.

SLOVAKIA

FRANCE

SWITZERLAND

AUSTRIA HUNGARY

MOLDOVA

ROMANIA

SLOVENIA

N

W   E

S

ANDORRA

CROATIA

Black Sea

SERBIA
AND
MONTENEGRO BULGARIA

PORTUGAL

SPAIN

MONACO

ITALY

BOSNIA AND
HERZEGOVINA

MACEDONIA

ALBANIA

TURKEY

GREECE

Mediterranean Sea

Population Cartogram of Europe

SWEDEN

NORWAY FINLAND

ESTONIA

LATVIA

LITHUANIA

DENMARK

POLAND

IRELAND UNITED
KINGDOM

NETHERLANDS

RUSSIA

GERMANY

BELARUS

ATLANTIC OCEAN

BELGIUM

CZECH
REP.

SLOVAKIA

UKRAINE

FRANCE

HUNGARY

MOLDOVA

AUSTRIA

SWITZERLAND

ROMANIA

SLOVENIA

CROATIA

SERBIA
AND
MONTENEGRO BULGARIA Black Sea

BOSNIA AND
HERZEGOVINA

PORTUGAL

SPAIN

ALBANIA

ITALY

GREECE

TURKEY

MACEDONIA

Mediterranean Sea

The Republic Weakens

DIRECTIONS Complete the organizer's descriptions of events and outcomes that led to the weakening of the Roman Republic.

Events	Outcomes
Wealthy and powerful Romans raise taxes and use enslaved people from conquered lands as free labor.	Roman farmers _____ _____ _____
Two brothers, _____ _____ _____ _____	Both men lose their lives. Rome is no longer ruled by law, but by force.
Two generals, _____ _____ _____ _____	Sulla wins the war and has himself declared dictator. He rules Rome for three years.
The triumvirate of Julius Caesar, Crassus, and Pompey agrees to share power over Rome.	Caesar's ambitions _____ _____ _____
Caesar captures Gaul and leads his army to Rome, where he declares himself dictator for life over all of Rome and its provinces.	Caesar _____ _____

Name _____   Date _____

Study Guide

DIRECTIONS Fill in the missing information in this summary. Use the terms below to help you complete the summary.

Lesson 1	Lesson 2	Lesson 3	Lesson 4
Romulus	patricians	Corinth	Pompey
Forum	tribunes	Roman Lake	reform
Tarquinius Priscus	republic	Carthage	assassinated
arable	consuls	provinces	Sulla
confederation		Italian Peninsula	Gaul

Lesson 1   The ancient Latins settled along the seven hills south of the

Tiber River on the Italian Peninsula. They found the region to be rich in

_____ land and to have a favorable location for trade and

protection from enemies.

　　The city of Rome became established as people moved down from the hills

to the flat land around the _____, which was used as a public

square. Legends say that the city was named after _____,

who was descended from Aeneas, a hero of the Trojan War.

　　The Romans adapted cultural ideas from the Greeks and the Etruscans. The

Etruscan _____ of 12 city-states eventually came to control

Rome, too. Legends say that when the Roman king died in about 616 B.C., the

Etruscan king _____ replaced him peacefully.

Lesson 2   An Etruscan tyrant later ruled Rome, and he was overthrown in

509 B.C. The Romans formed a new government, a _____ that

allowed citizens to elect their leaders. Their tripartite government, which was

designed so that power was shared and balanced, was made up of two

CALIFORNIA STANDARDS HSS 6.7, 6.7.1, 6.7.2, 6.7.3, 6.7.4   (continued)

Lesson 2 *(continued)* _____, the Senate, and the assemblies.

The Roman Republic had two main classes—the _____, who were wealthy landowners, and the plebeians, who were soldiers, farmers, craftworkers, and merchants. The plebeians later gained the right to elect _____ to represent them.

Lesson 3 Rome's power grew. By 272 B.C., the Romans controlled the _____. Conflict over trade routes in the Mediterranean led to the Punic Wars between Rome and _____. By 146 B.C., Rome controlled _____ in Africa. During battles with the Greeks, the Romans destroyed _____. By 133 B.C., Rome ruled nearly all of the region. The Mediterranean Sea became known as the _____.

Lesson 4 Serious problems arose within Rome's government. Tribunes who attempted to _____ unfair laws were killed, and Rome came to be ruled by force. A struggle for power created a civil war, and General _____ declared himself dictator. In 60 B.C., Rome was ruled by a triumvirate of powerful generals made up of Crassus, _____, and Julius Caesar. Caesar planned to expand Roman territories, and he led an army that captured _____ in the region that is now France. Caesar returned to Rome and named himself dictator for life, but he was _____ a month later.

READING SOCIAL STUDIES: DRAW CONCLUSIONS

(Focus Skill) The Early Romans

DIRECTIONS Complete this graphic organizer to show that you can draw conclusions about ancient Rome.

Draw Conclusions

Evidence

The Roman region had arable land.

Knowledge

People settle in places where there are good farming conditions.

Conclusion

_____

_____

_____

From Republic to Empire

DIRECTIONS Complete the flowchart to tell about events in Rome after Caesar's assassination. Then answer the question that follows.

The Second Triumvirate—42 B.C.

After the assassination of Julius Caesar and the defeat of Brutus and Cassius, Rome is ruled by the Second Triumvirate of Octavian, Mark Antony, and Lepidus.

⬇

A Plan to Overthrow Octavian—36 B.C.

When Lepidus attempts to overthrow Octavian, _____

_____

_____

⬇

Octavian Conquers Egypt—31 B.C.

Unhappy with the rule of Antony and Cleopatra VII, Octavian _____

_____

_____

⬇

The Transition from Republic to Empire—27 B.C.

As the first emperor of Rome, Octavian is renamed Augustus. Rome has transitioned

from being a republic to an empire, meaning that _____

_____

How was Octavian the heir of Julius Caesar? How were they alike in what they wanted

for Rome? _____

_____

_____

_____

CALIFORNIA STANDARDS HSS 6.7, 6.7.1, 6.7.3, 6.7.4   (continued)

Name _____ Date _____

DIRECTIONS Complete the organizer to describe the diversity of the Roman Empire under Augustus. Then answer the questions that follow.

Diversity in the Roman Empire

Geographic Regions	Cultures	Spoken Languages
_____	_____	_____
_____	_____	_____
_____	_____	_____
_____	_____	_____
_____	_____	_____

Augustus allowed the provinces to keep their own cultures. How did this help him rule and unify the Roman Empire?

_____

_____

Augustus granted citizenship to free men in the provinces. Why do you think being a Roman citizen was important to those in the provinces?

_____

_____

Skills: Compare Historical Maps

DIRECTIONS Study the maps below, which show the city of Rome in different time periods. Use the maps to complete the activities on the following page.

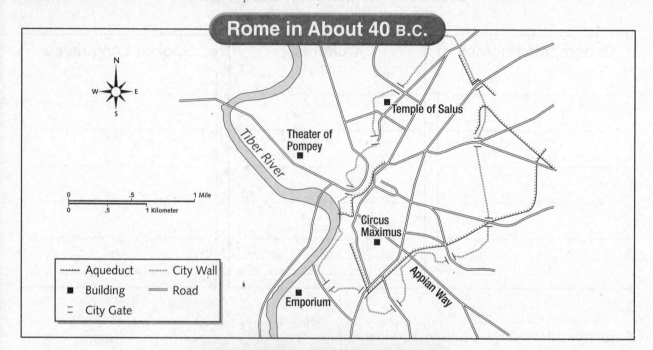

Rome in About 40 B.C.

- Tiber River
- Temple of Salus
- Theater of Pompey
- Circus Maximus
- Appian Way
- Emporium

Scale: 0 — .5 — 1 Mile / 0 — .5 — 1 Kilometer

Legend:
- ⋯⋯ Aqueduct
- ■ Building
- = City Gate
- ⋯⋯ City Wall
- — Road

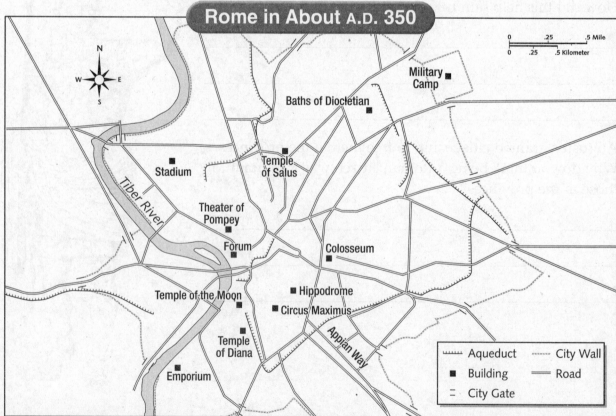

Rome in About A.D. 350

Scale: 0 — .25 — .5 Mile / 0 — .25 — .5 Kilometer

- Military Camp
- Baths of Diocletian
- Stadium
- Temple of Salus
- Tiber River
- Theater of Pompey
- Forum
- Colosseum
- Temple of the Moon
- Hippodrome
- Circus Maximus
- Temple of Diana
- Appian Way
- Emporium

Legend:
- ⋯⋯ Aqueduct
- ■ Building
- = City Gate
- ⋯⋯ City Wall
- — Road

CALIFORNIA STANDARDS HSS 6.7, 6.7.1, 6.7.3; CS 3

(continued)

© Harcourt

Name _____ Date _____

1 How many years apart are the time periods on the maps? _____

2 In 40 B.C., was the Theater of Pompey inside or outside the city wall?

_____

3 In 40 B.C., was the Emporium inside or outside the city wall?

_____

4 By A.D. 350, was the Emporium inside or outside the city wall?

_____

5 By what year was the Circus Maximus built? _____

6 By what year was the Temple of Diana built? _____

7 The Romans built systems of aqueducts, or bridges and canals that carried water, from the Tiber River to the city. Why do you think the Romans had expanded the

systems of aqueducts by A.D. 350? _____

_____

8 Which physical feature can be found on both maps? By A.D. 350, how had Roman control of this physical feature changed?

_____

_____

_____

Times of Peace

DIRECTIONS Imagine that you are a soldier in the Roman Empire's army. Describe the reforms Augustus has put into place, and tell what you think about them.

_____

_____

_____

_____

_____

DIRECTIONS Complete the organizer to show how roads and rivers were used by the Roman Empire. Then answer the question that follows.

Roads and Rivers

Trade:	Military:	Communication:
_____	_____	_____
_____	_____	_____
_____	_____	_____
_____	_____	_____
_____	_____	_____

Why did Augustus create a standard currency for the Roman Empire in 24 B.C.?

_____

_____

_____

CALIFORNIA STANDARDS HSS 6.7.3, 6.7.4   (continued)

138 ▪ Homework and Practice Book   Use after reading Chapter 13, Lesson 2, pages 514–519.

Name _____   Date _____

DIRECTIONS Match each Roman emperor from the box with his description below. Write each name on the line provided.

Trajan	Nero	Claudius	Hadrian	Marcus Aurelius
Tiberius	Nerva	Vespasian	Titus	Antoninus Pius

1 _____ This general ruled for 10 years and was one of the first emperors who was not related to Julius Caesar.

2 _____ He improved the lives of the poor and was tolerant of other religions, including Judaism and Christianity.

3 _____ The work of this emperor centered on providing defense for the lands of the Roman Empire.

4 _____ The son of Augustus, he made many enemies and took away some of the rights of the Romans.

5 _____ Although he was not a native of Rome, he was well-liked and brought the Roman Empire to its greatest size.

6 _____ Part of Britain was brought under the control of the Roman Empire during his rule.

7 _____ He was greatly disliked by his people, and much of Rome was destroyed in a great fire during his reign.

8 _____ This emperor faced invasions and ruled the Roman Empire during a deadly plague.

9 _____ After a rebellion in Judaea, he destroyed the city of Jerusalem in A.D. 70.

10 _____ As the adopted son of Hadrian, he ruled the prosperous Roman Empire well for a long time.

Everyday Life in Ancient Rome

DIRECTIONS Write *T* next to the statements that are true and *F* next to the statements that are false. Then answer the questions that follow.

1 _____ Most gladiators in ancient Rome were military heroes.

2 _____ Most people in ancient Rome lived in apartment buildings that were crowded, noisy, dirty, and often unsafe.

3 _____ The population of Rome was about the same as that of other cities in the Roman Empire, such as Athens and Alexandria.

4 _____ Aqueducts were built to supply water from a natural source to cities and towns in the Roman Empire.

5 _____ The phrase "bread and circuses" refers to how rulers of ancient Rome supplied free food and entertainment to people in order to win their support.

6 _____ Wealthy citizens had to use public baths and fountains to get fresh water.

7 _____ Nearly all Roman citizens enjoyed the many meats and special foods that were imported from different parts of the empire.

8 _____ Rome served as the model for other cities in the Roman Empire.

9 How was the Roman Empire dependent on slavery?

_____

_____

_____

10 If you had been an ordinary citizen in the Roman Empire, would you have **preferred** to live in the city or in the country? Tell why.

_____

_____

_____

CALIFORNIA STANDARDS HSS 6.7, 6.7.3, 6.7.8

Skills: Read Editorial Cartoons

DIRECTIONS Answer the following questions about editorial cartoons.

1 What do editorial cartoons usually present?

_____

2 How does knowing how to read editorial cartoons help you understand political and cultural issues?

_____

_____

DIRECTIONS In the space provided, draw your own editorial cartoon about the Roman Empire. Pick a topic from below.

Roman Taxation	Everyday Life in the City
Trade and Currency	Octavian Is Named Augustus Caesar

3 What symbols or details did you use to present your point of view?

_____

_____

CALIFORNIA STANDARDS HSS 6.7, 6.7.3, 6.7.4; HR 5

Name _____   Date _____

Study Guide

DIRECTIONS Fill in the missing information in this summary. Use the terms below to help you complete the summary.

Lesson 1	Lesson 2	Lesson 3
Mark Antony	currency	census
respect	Marcus Aurelius	gladiators
Cleopatra	Trajan	slaves
unity	Tiberius	city
Lepidus	trade routes	aqueducts
Julius Caesar	reforms	country

Lesson 1   After a civil war, three men known as the Second Triumvirate ruled

Rome together. They were Lepidus, _____, and Octavian, the

heir of _____. Soon, conflicts among these leaders emerged.

Octavian removed _____ from power when Octavian learned

of a plan to overthrow him. Later, after Octavian defeated Mark Antony and

_____, he gained control of Egypt and ruled the entire

Mediterranean world.

In 27 B.C., Octavian was given the title Augustus by the Senate to signify

_____. Ruling over many diverse peoples and cultures,

Augustus aimed to bring _____ and stability to Rome.

CALIFORNIA STANDARDS HSS 6.7, 6.7.1, 6.7.3, 6.7.4   *(continued)*

142 ■ **Homework and Practice Book**   Use after reading Chapter 13, pages 506–525.

Lesson 2   Augustus ruled the Roman Empire for more than 40 years. He

enacted _____ that improved the lives of those in the

military and established a standard _____ for the empire.

He repaired and extended roads that strengthened the exchange of goods and

communication along _____ .

　　　After his death, Augustus was succeeded by his son,

_____ . Not long afterward, the Roman Empire entered

a period of instability. Beginning in A.D. 96, the empire entered another

period, known as the time of the Five Good Emperors. Under the emperor

_____ , the Roman Empire grew to its largest size. In A.D. 161,

the empire faced new problems. Under _____ , Rome's

stability was weakened by a serious plague and outside invasions.

Lesson 3   Most Romans were poor, but the wealthy Romans lived in luxury.

In the _____ , most people lived in crowded, noisy apartment

buildings. Wealthy citizens enjoyed lavish homes and goods imported from

all over the empire. Water was supplied to public baths and fountains by a

system of _____ . In the _____ , most

people were farmers. In both places, much of the day-to-day work was done by

_____ .

　　　The records of the Roman _____ indicate that about

1 million people lived in Rome at the time of Augustus. People enjoyed a

variety of popular entertainment, including chariot races, fighting matches with

_____ , and plays.

Name _____ Date _____

READING SOCIAL STUDIES: DRAW CONCLUSIONS

Focus
Skill

The Roman Empire

DIRECTIONS Complete this graphic organizer to show that you can draw conclusions about the Roman Empire.

Draw Conclusions

Evidence

Roman officials made Latin the official language of the Roman Empire.

Knowledge

_____
_____
_____
_____

Conclusion

Communication across the Roman Empire grew.

CALIFORNIA STANDARDS HSS 6.7, 6.7.3, 6.7.4

Use after reading Chapter 13, pages 506–525.

Religion in the Roman Empire

DIRECTIONS Complete the sentences to tell about religion in the Roman Empire. Then answer the questions that follow.

1 The Romans believed that their gods had human forms, an idea borrowed from

_____

_____

2 Some other cultures that influenced Roman religious beliefs included

_____

3 Because religion was a part of the Roman government, Rome's emperor

_____

_____

4 All Romans were required by law to _____

5 The Romans believed that failure to worship their gods through offerings and

rituals would _____

6 Many other religions and philosophies were followed in the Roman Empire, including

_____

_____

7 Even though the Jewish people within the Roman Empire did not worship Roman

gods, they were allowed to practice their religion because _____

_____

8 The Judaean king Herod showed his loyalty to the Roman government by

_____

9 What do you think was the main reason why Jews revolted several times against

Roman rule? _____

_____

10 Why do you think the emperor Hadrian expelled all Jews from Jerusalem?

_____

_____

CALIFORNIA STANDARDS HSS 6.7, 6.7.5

The Beginnings of Christianity

DIRECTIONS Use the names and terms from the box to complete the **sentences** about the beginnings of Christianity in the Roman Empire.

parables	Messiah	apostles	Nazareth	Herod the Great
disciples	Gospels	Paul	persecution	resurrection

1 A major source of conflict about Jesus during his time centered around **whether** he was the long-awaited _____ who would lead the Jewish **people.**

2 The main sources that tell about the life of Jesus and his teachings are called **the** _____, the first four books of the New Testament of the Bible.

3 The story of the Good Samaritan is an example of one of the _____ that Jesus used to teach people about moral ways to live.

4 At the time of Jesus' birth, _____ was the ruler of Judaea.

5 The men who spread the word throughout the Roman Empire about Jesus **and** his importance were the _____.

6 When Jesus' parents returned to Judaea, they settled in _____ **and** raised Jesus in the traditions of the Jewish religion.

7 The 12 men who traveled with Jesus were known as the _____.

8 After a Jewish man named Saul became convinced that Jesus was the true **leader** of the Jewish people, he changed his name to _____ **and dedicated** his life to telling others about Jesus.

9 Jesus' followers spread the story of his _____ after he had **been** put to death.

10 As Christians spread the word of their new religion, they faced _____ for their beliefs from Roman leaders.

CALIFORNIA STANDARDS HSS 6.7, 6.7.6, 6.7.7; HI 1, 2   *(continued)*

Name _____ Date _____

Answer the following questions about the life and teachings of Jesus and the rise of Christianity in the Roman Empire.

1 Why did Jesus' parents go to Egypt from Judaea? _____

_____

_____

2 What were the main teachings that Jesus and his followers spread?

_____

_____

_____

_____

3 Why was Jesus a source of conflict among the Jews?

_____

_____

_____

4 Why did Roman leaders feel threatened by Jesus?

_____

_____

_____

5 How did the ideas of Christianity spread after Jesus was put to death? Why were these ideas still a threat to Roman leaders?

_____

_____

_____

_____

_____

Skills: Compare Graphs

DIRECTIONS Study the graphs below about Italy from 1950 to 2000. Use the graphs to complete the activities that follow.

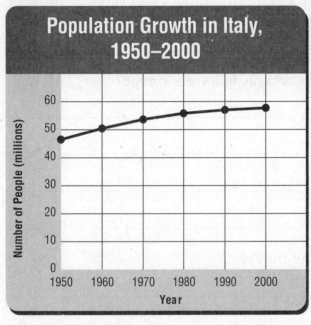

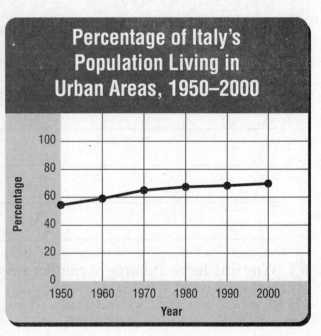

Source: United Nations World Population Prospects Population Database

1 How did Italy's population change from 1950 to 2000?

_____

2 What trend do you see in Italy's population growth from 1980 to 2000?

_____

3 What percentage of Italy's population lived in cities in 1950? In 2000?

_____

4 Did the urban percentage of Italy's population increase dramatically between 1980 and 2000? _____

5 Use the first graph to make a prediction about Italy's population in 2020.

_____

_____

CALIFORNIA STANDARDS HSS 6.7; CS 3

Christianity and the Romans

DIRECTIONS Answer the two questions about the growth of Christianity in the Roman Empire. Then use the organizer to tell about how Constantine the Great became a Christian and supported Christianity in the Roman Empire during the early A.D. 300s.

What was Emperor Trajan's policy toward Christians?

_____

_____

_____

What were two reasons that Christianity had an appeal to people in the Roman Empire?

_____

_____

_____

	Has a vision in A.D. 312:
Constantine the Great and Christianity	_____ _____ _____
	Issues the Edict of Milan in A.D. 313: _____ _____ _____
	Becomes baptized in A.D. 337: _____ _____ _____

CALIFORNIA STANDARDS HSS 6.7, 6.7.3, 6.7.6, 6.7.7; HI 2   *(continued)*

Name _____ Date _____

Complete the organizer to tell how Christianity developed in the Roman Empire and how authority and power became established.

Theodosius I

The first Christian churches in the Roman Empire are

_____

_____

The emperor Constantine gives Christians the right to

_____

_____

In A.D. 391, the emperor Theodosius

_____

_____

The Roman government provides _____

_____

Bishops in each city become powerful because _____

_____

As the bishop of the city of Rome, the pope _____

_____

Skills: Identify Causes and Effects

DIRECTIONS Reread each section from your textbook, and use the information to complete the cause-and-effect charts.

In A.D. 391, Emperor Theodosius I made Christianity the official religion of the Roman Empire. Christianity replaced the old state religion, with its many gods and goddesses. Theodosius banned the practice of the old religion and closed its temples.

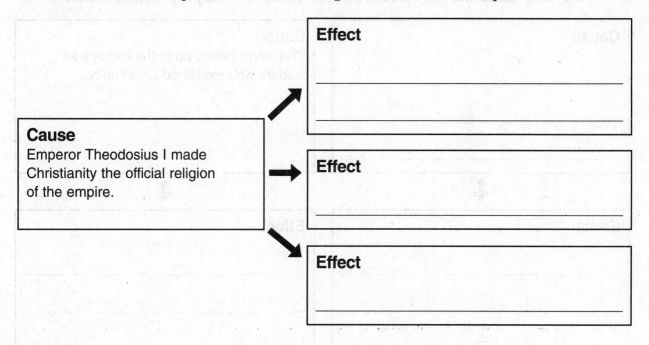

Effect

_____

_____

Cause
Emperor Theodosius I made Christianity the official religion of the empire.

Effect

_____

_____

Effect

_____

_____

Now the Roman government built large churches to replace the old temples. Church leaders managed these large churches and the money the government provided for them. The most powerful of these leaders were the bishops.

Cause
New churches were constructed to replace the old temples.

Cause

_____

_____

Effect

_____

_____

CALIFORNIA STANDARDS HSS 6.7, 6.7.7; HI 2

(continued)

Name _____ Date _____

Each large city had a church along with a bishop to take care of church business. Since they controlled money given to the churches, bishops often became rich and powerful. Christians looked up to the bishops as leaders who explained Christianity and told **them** what was right and what was wrong. This gave the bishops political power. Rulers knew that if they displeased the bishops, the bishops could turn the people against them.

Cause

_____

_____

_____

Cause
Christians looked up to the bishops as leaders who explained Christianity.

⬇

Effect

_____

_____

_____

Effect

_____

_____

_____

Effect

_____

_____

_____

_____

What two elements gave the bishops so much power? _____

_____

Use after reading Chapter 14, Skill Lesson, pages 556–557.

Name _____ Date _____

Rome's Legacy

DIRECTIONS Complete the organizer to tell how Roman influences are still felt in the world today. Then answer the question that follows.

Language

_____

_____

_____

_____

Government and Law

_____

_____

_____

_____

Literature and the Arts

The works of Cicero, Tacitus, Virgil, Horace, and Ovid are still studied today. Sculptures, mosaics, and other artworks still inspire and influence us today.

Legacies of the Roman Empire

Architecture

The Romans built on the ideas of other cultures to create buildings, like basilicas, that are still commonly used today.

Science

_____

_____

_____

Technology

_____

_____

_____

What do you think was the most important contribution from the Roman Empire to today's world? Explain your ideas.

_____

_____

_____

_____

CALIFORNIA STANDARDS HSS 6.7, 6.7.8; HI 2

Name _____ Date _____

Study Guide

DIRECTIONS Fill in the missing information in this summary. Use the terms below to help you complete the summary.

Lesson 1	Lesson 2	Lesson 3	Lesson 4
Hadrian	persecution	Theodosius	Latin
Greeks	Gospels	pope	Ptolemy
sect	crucifixion	bishop	basilica
Augustus	Messiah	salvation	Virgil
Herod the Great	disciples	Constantine the Great	justice

Lesson 1 The ancient Romans adopted their religious ideas from the

_____ . The Romans built temples to honor and make offer-

ings to their gods. Religion became part of Rome's government. Emperor

_____ believed that honoring their gods would help unite

the empire, but he allowed other religions to be practiced in the Roman

Empire, including Judaism. As king of Judaea, _____

rebuilt the Jewish Temple in Jerusalem. Conflicts over religious beliefs

worsened over time, and the Jews rebelled. Finally, the Roman emperor

_____ expelled all the Jewish people from Jerusalem. During

this time, Christianity, which had begun as a _____ of

Judaism, became a separate religion.

Lesson 2 The _____ in the New Testament of the Bible

tell about the life and teachings of Jesus. He and his _____

traveled through Judaea and taught his ideas about God's forgiveness and

loving one another. Because many people believed that Jesus was the

🐻 **CALIFORNIA STANDARDS HSS 6.7, 6.7.5, 6.7.6, 6.7.7, 6.7.8** *(continued)*

154 ▪ Homework and Practice Book   Use after reading Chapter 14, pages 536–561.

Lesson 2 *(continued)* _____, he was seen as a threat by some Jewish and Roman leaders. After his _____, Jesus' followers told of his resurrection. While many Christians suffered _____ because of their beliefs, Christianity grew and spread in the Roman Empire.

Lesson 3   Christianity grew in popularity because it accepted all people, and its promise of _____ appealed to many people. When _____ became a Christian and later issued the Edict of Milan, the religion became accepted throughout the Roman Empire. In A.D. 391, Emperor _____ made Christianity the empire's official religion. Soon churches were constructed, and each one was managed by a _____. Over time, the religious leader of the city of Rome, the _____, became the most powerful of all.

Lesson 4   Modern civilizations are influenced by the Roman Empire. Many languages are based on _____, and nearly half of all English words come from it. Many Roman writers, such as Horace and _____, are studied today.

Many governments have been modeled on the Roman Republic, and its ideas about law and _____ are used in countries around the world. Likewise, the contributions of Roman scientists such as _____ and Galen influence modern scientists.

While the ancient Roman architects borrowed and added to ideas from other cultures, the Roman _____ is now a common style for Christian churches. The worlds of art, culture, science, government, and law have all benefited from the legacy of the Roman Empire.

READING SOCIAL STUDIES: DRAW CONCLUSIONS

 The Legacies of Rome

DIRECTIONS Complete this graphic organizer to show that you can draw conclusions about the legacies of Rome.

Draw Conclusions

Evidence

The Romans invented concrete.

Knowledge

_____

_____

_____

_____

Conclusion

The legacy of Rome lives on in today's society.

CALIFORNIA STANDARDS HSS 6.7, 6.7.8

156 ■ Homework and Practice Book   Use after reading Chapter 14, pages 536–561.